SYMPATHETIC
LEADERSHIP
CYBERNETICS

SYMPATHETIC LEADERSHIP CYBERNETICS

Serving Organizations Through Shepherd Management and Servant Leadership

Hollis L. Green, ThD, PhD

GlobalEdAdvancePress™

www.globaledadvance.org

SYMPAHETIC LEADERSHIP CYBERNETICS
Serving Organizations Through Shepherd Management and Servant Leadership

Copyright © 2010 by Hollis L. Green

Library of Congress Control Number: 2010910950
Green, Hollis L., 1933 –
Sympathetic Leadership Cybernetics
ISBN 978-1-935434-52-8

Subject Codes and Description: 1;REL.071000: Religion:
Leadership; 2: EDU. 032000 Education: Leadership; 3:
EDU.001000: Education: Administration-General

Printed in the USA.

Cover design by Barton Green

The Press does not have ownership of the contents of a book; this
is the author's work and the author owns the copyright. All theory,
concepts, constructs, and perspectives are those of the author and not
necessarily the Press. They are presented for open and free discussion
of the issues involved. All comments and feedback should be directed
to the Email: [comments4author@aol.com] and the comments will be
forwarded to the author for response.

Published by
GLOBALEDADVANCE PRESS
WWW.GLOBALEDADVANCE.ORG

Dedicated
To the memory of

Col. Creed F. Bates

Who pushed many toward
Honorable leadership roles.

.

TABLE OF CONTENTS

Introduction

A Creation of Human Culture

The traditional constructs of management and leadership were the creation of human culture of past generations; consequently, these definitions derived from past constructs are limited in application and adequacy for today. The existent literature is mostly secular, and the customary definitions and understanding of management and leadership functions as practiced in global corporations may not be sufficiently grounded for nonprofits, NGOs, or faith-based organizations.

Although nonprofits and faith-based groups may benefit from much of the research about organizations, the management and leadership of not-for-profit corporations, educational institutions, church denominations, and Para-church groups, require a deeper understanding of the essential constructs that inform management and leadership in an organized and structured community. Without this understanding, the development of corporately shared community life may be limited. Worse still, some may attempt to operate a not-for-profit enterprise as if it were a money-making business. One must remember that being in the nonprofit sector means the organization is serving a particular need in society and often many of the staff are volunteers or are working for reduced pay. This requires a particular mindset and predisposition to behave in a manner appropriate for a service or faith-based organization.

Words of the past may not adequately inform the present as to (1) the passions of persons, (2) the complexity of groups, (3) the forms and use of power in organizational life, and (4) the dynamics of positional authority and personal influence. This book is about organizations and leaders today.   Words and thought forms inherent in the terms used by organizations are misunderstood by an urban, complex world; such as, boss, executive, foreman, landlord, principal, chief, owner, superintendent, overseer, or bishop. These words may have negative connotations for some people in a modern organization and particularly in the nonprofit sector.

The intention of the author is to clarify the attitudes and actions of managers working with positional authority and those functioning in organizational leadership roles primarily through personal influence.   It is not an exhaustive text, but designed to stimulate the interest of serious students in a particular aspect of management and leadership required in the nonprofit sector.   Most of the concepts and constructs in the text, particularly "sympathetic" and "cybernetics," were used in graduate classes for the past three decades. Many students were convinced that other socially responsible institutions and organizations could profit from the concepts and constructs presented in the text.

Author's Note

This book is based on a graduate course taught for several years. A syllabus outline is presented in Chapter Eleven. For those who wish to teach or research the text, a searchable CD is available as well as a PowerPoint presentation. These may be ordered directly from GlobalEdAdvancePress, Lone Mountain Office, 345 Barton Road, Dayton, TN 37321-7635. Just send payment of $9.95 for the searchable CD and $4.95 for the PowerPointPresentation. Free shipping in the USA.

At the end of Chapter Twelve, Selected Resources and Bibliography, are four additional books that may assist those teaching or taking this course. These books and others published by the PRESS may be ordered from www. globaledadvance.org/bookstore. Free shipping within the USA is your discount.

Transformational Leadership in Education
Interpreting an Author's Words
Remedial and Surrogate Parenting
How to Build a Better Spouse Trap

CHAPTER ONE

Sympathetic Leadership Cybernetics

A Sympathetic System

A sympathetic system is sophisticated and appears to be complicated whether it is the human antonomical nervous system or the automatic workings inside a computer; however, when one understands the system it appears entirely different. These systems, although complex, are not complicated when one comprehends the inner mechanism. Knowing how the system works makes the difference. When one works with the system, a synergy or "working together" develops that simplifies the process. For example, when one combines word processing skills with the mechanism of a PC, a real synergy occurs. The sympathetic cybernetic approach to leadership can remove much of the complication and enable practitioners to appear more sophisticated in approaching issues in managing and/or leading others.

Synergy

Synergy occurs when two or more forces work, so the combined effort is greater than the sum of the individual efforts. Synergy requires an understanding of how the system actually works. Understanding requires both discernment and comprehension that permits a reconciliation of differences; thus, it becomes sympathetic. This is what leadership is all about: the ability to influence both individuals and circumstances based on a sameness of feeling. In fact, individuals are influenced to change and in turn these changed individuals make the necessary changes in the environment of the organization.

Early in my professional life there were two plaques on my desk: "Faith without works is dead!" and "Ideas are funny little things, they don't work unless you do!" Also, I learned the old saying "Prayer changes things" did not provide the whole proposition. People received the wrong idea from a fragment of the adage. Many assumed they could simply pray a few words and do nothing themselves, and some divine power would step in and fix the problem. However, prayer is much like an idea: it doesn't work unless you personally do something.

The actual construct of the proverb was "Prayer changes people and people change things." The same is true in the arena of leadership. Leaders must pay attention to the "people to people" aspect of the administrative process. It is the people that change things not an all powerful leader. Therefore, those in places of leadership should remember the obvious variation of "minister" and "administer." The construct of "minister" relates to serving the needs of an individual; while the word "administer" suggests a broader corporate meaning of managing the affairs of others. An awareness of both serving the needs of the individual and caring for the larger needs of the organization come together in the conception of sympathetic leadership cybernetics.

Theoretical and Applied Analysis

Theoretical and applied analysis of organizational leadership provides an understanding of the deeper constructs of behavior required to manage and lead an organization. The conflict between coherent management and common leadership may be overcome through administrative consciousness of the interconnectedness of all aspects of an organization. At times, new words are needed to shake off the lethargy of the past and become a dynamic and functioning force in organizational life.

One of the leadership words used in my graduate classes for many years is "cybernetics" dealing with a feedback system that must be understood by those who would either lead or manage an organized group.   Another word that needs to be added to the present mix is "sympathetic."   This word can move managers and leaders into the affective domain where one can feel the same thing that others are feeling. This sense of sameness and the ability to share the common feelings that provide affinity between persons is a necessary ingredient to contemporary leadership.   The affective domain permits action based on feeling with others, rather than viewing the situation from the top of the administrative tower. The science of cybernetics and the construct of a sympathetic system combine to provide leadership with a guiding framework to influence the actions of individuals and groups in an organizational setting based on a mutual understanding of people and conditions.

Notwithstanding contemporary concepts, the constructs that inform the not-for-profit view of management and leadership are rooted in the distant past. These words may only be fully grasped in the context of a nonprofit organization, provided a few ancient scriptural words are understood and made operational as they inform management and leadership. The pristine words; such as, sheep, shepherd and servant still have value and positive meaning.   Improvement is required to provide a nonprofit perspective of leadership and management relevant to the Twenty-first Century. A look at these key words is required to fully understand the function of sympathetic leadership cybernetics as they relate to shepherd management and servant leadership.

Ability to Influence People

People assume that placing a person in a given position will change things; however, people must be changed before an organization can change. The person placed in position to utilize personal influence must be tuned to the affective domain and base all action on that understanding. The chief requirement of leadership is the ability to influence people to follow one voluntarily toward stated goals. Thus, one can clearly see the fallacy in using only positional power without the sympathetic cybernetic function.

Authentic leadership will use all four of the essential leadership elements: vision, courage, integrity, and perseverance. A prerequisite element must be added: knowledge of how organizations develop and grow. Unless a proposed leader understands how the organization develops and grows, utilizing the other essential aspects will be futile. A precondition to utilizing vision, courage, integrity, and perseverance is the basic knowledge of how organizations mature and expand.

Essential Leadership Elements

It is difficult to explain how the individual brain works, how the inner workings of a computer function, or how people behave in organizations. The field of cybernetics deals with the science of complex electronic calculating machines and the human nervous system in an attempt to explain the nature of the brain. The term "cybernetics" comes from the Greek, *kybernetes*, meaning "helmsman." Most leaders are so far removed from the seafaring age that even the concept of "helmsman" escapes the vocabulary. A "helmsman" was "the person at the helm; the one who steered the ship." The "helm" is defined as "the complete steering gear, including the wheel or tiller, rudder, etc." In addition, the helmsman must know the crew, the currents, the winds, and the nature of the waters in which the ship is moving. Making the translation and/or application to leadership is not difficult. To steer is to direct the course or progress of the organization. To manage an organization or to lead people in the organization, one must be a helmsman.

Sympathetic cybernetics can assist leaders in a clear understanding of how organizations mature and progress. Leadership often considers a principled and practical operation sufficient to guarantee growth and progress. This attitude obstructs the inherent factors of growth and causes the organization to be content with mediocrity. A willingness to settle for something less than the best causes an organization to suffer from predictable disease and to become strangulated in vital areas of growth and progress. The willingness to settle for mediocre operations also brings about a lack of global perspective and produces neglect in the areas of outreach, recruiting and funding.

Leadership cybernetics simply speaks to the control factors in management and leadership of an organized enterprise. Management and leadership suggest the leader understands the environment and the people and has the ability to guide or steer the organization through good and bad times with a clear vision.

Vision.   A strategic visualization of the future needs of the organization and the ability to develop an agenda to reach certain goals. A dream has no agenda; a goal has a vision with a clear agenda, and a feasible plan that deals with the realities of getting from the existent to the next level of achievement and advancement for the organization.   This vision must be articulated with a certain audacity.

Courage.   A leader must possess a confident audacity and fluency of speech that enables a clear articulation of a visualization that would alter the existing state of affairs.

There is no substitute for courage. Courage does not mean that one acts or behaves without a measure of fear; it is the ability to function in spite of reasonable fears. Valor without integrity creates a less than honorable situation.

Integrity. A certain reliability and veracity is required to convince others to follow one toward strategic goals. A leader speaks the truth and maintains an obvious sincerity without artificiality. This gives authenticity to the person and breeds trust and loyalty which convince others to follow in spite of known difficulties.

Perseverance. There must be a sense of urgency demonstrated in both tone and action about the journey toward stated goals. Difficulties must not dissuade an attitude of firmness about the plan of action, and a determined resolve to progress toward group goals. Such resolve is required to secure volunteers who will in turn facilitate the plan. Perseverance can assure a firm insistence on the vital steps in the plan of action as long the S-curve of growth is noticeably understood and appreciated.

Collegial Model of Leadership in Education
It is common in business and industry for the Chair of the Board to also be the Chief Executive Officer (CEO) of the Corporation while someone else is assigned the responsibility of operating the company (COO). In the field of higher education, accreditation commissions require that the Board Chair not be the CEO of an educational institution. The positions are divided because education is a different kind of operation. In higher education, the term Chief Executive Officer does not mean the same as in business and industry. The CEO has executive authority, but is expected to work with other officers in the institution based on general guidelines and policies of the Board.

In the case of education, the Chair of the Board inspects the general operation of the institution on behalf of the Board to verify that approved policies and procedures are followed, but does not attempt to micromanage the process. The CEO is accountable to the Board for the day-to-day operation in cooperation and consultation with the other chief officers.

In secondary schools, there is a Superintendent and a Principal with different responsibilities and accountability to the Board. Colleges and Universities often have both a Chancellor and a President with different responsibilities and accountability. In addition to the two offices above, in higher education there is also a Chief Academic Officer (CAO), a Chief Financial Officer (CFO), and at times a Chief Operating Officer (COO). When an individual is designated as CEO, that person does not have total authority in the institution because of the other individuals who also have the title of "chief." There must be participatory leadership with one individual making a final decision. Therefore, it is proposed that institutions of higher education bring these offices together into an Operations Committee with the CEO as Chair in what is called the "Collegial Model of Leadership in Education."

The Collegial Model is excellent for a nonprofit, NGO's or educational institution. Collegial leadership is in contrast to business or bureaucratic leadership. In the Collegial Model the CEO is considered the "first among equals" in an organization run by professionals. Essentially, the collegial model advances the dynamic of consensus in a community of leaders. The basic role of the CEO in this model is not so much to command as to listen, not so much to lead as to gather expert judgments, not so much to manage as to facilitate, not so much to order but to persuade and negotiate.

A CEO in this model needs professional and educational skills to ensure high esteem by colleagues. Talent in interpersonal dynamics is also needed to achieve consensus in organizational decision-making. The objective is to create a harmonious atmosphere in which the individuals in "chief" positions may work together with a cooperative spirit based on general guidelines and policies approved by the Board. The persons filling the chief roles should work together in an Operations Committee which the CEO chairs.

The person designated as CEO by the Board would moderate the Operations Committee function and maintain record of decisions for Board review. The Operations Committee should manage the general operations of the Institution and together be responsible for the programs, administrative policies, business affairs, institutional advancement, and special projects related to the life of the institution. In particular, the Operations Committee will oversee the budgetary process and present an annual budget and audit to the Board for review and approval. This type of leadership is modest and realistic. Such a leader does not stand alone, since other professionals in the organization share the burden of decision. Negotiation and consensus building are the strengths of such a leader. Since other "chief" officers of the institution serve on the Operations Committee, the CEO will have wise counsel concerning executive decisions that must be made.

Study and Review Questions for Chapter One

1. What is the difference between a complicated and a sophisticated system?

2. What happens when two or more forces work together to form a synergy?

3. What is left out of the saying "Prayer changes things?"

4. What does interconnectedness relate to organizations and leaders?

5. Discuss the Greek meaning of cybernetics.

6. Relate sympathetic to leadership of a nonprofit organization.

7. When one discusses the essential elements of leadership as vision, courage, integrity, and perseverance, what is missing?

8. Discuss the Collegial Model of Leadership.

CHAPTER TWO

S-Curve of Organizational Growth

S-Curve of Growth

An understanding of the S-curve of growth, that all living organisms and organizations exhibit is essential to comprehending the inner workings of an organization. The S-curve of growth (See Figure 2.1) has three phases: a period called the lag phase (I) when preparation is being made for growth. The period of actual growth called exponential or logarithmic phase (II). This period of rapid growth climaxed in maximum efficiency and usually gives way to a healthy development through a constructive coordination of differing facets of the organization into a uniform whole. At this point in development, a stationary phase (III) usually develops because of the effort of the organization to survive. When the crisis is not met, the energies and resources normally used for outreach and expansion are re-channeled into the development of institutional design to maintain *status quo*; thus, the leveling off period is entered, when growth ceases and the size stabilizes. This is usually called the stationary phase or institutionalization phase and is most critical.

Sometimes in the standard development scheme of organizations the dynamic structure of growth is frustrated and the automatic nature of rejuvenation fails to work. The structures are modified progressively by processes operating within the organization as it evolves into a stable institution.

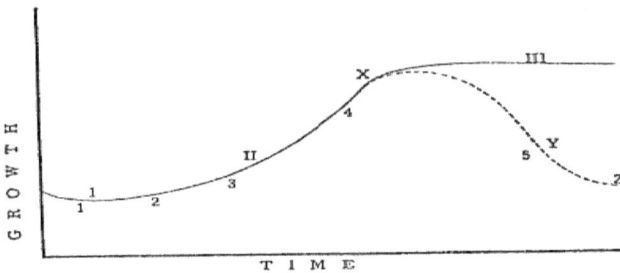

Figure 2.1 – Diagram of the normal growth curve of an organization: I-lag phase, II-logarithmic phase, III-stationary phase, X-point of crisis. Y-decreased population. Z-fixed size below potential. Numbers 1-5 are the same as Figure 1. 2.

Provided the organization survives, more formal rules are increasingly imposed on the organizational constituency. This process produces a vicious cycle that impairs the effectiveness of the organization. The sociologists claim that if the organization survives the early developing years the constituency numbers normally increase and the property becomes more aesthetic. There are at least five anticipated stages in this development that leadership must understand.
(See Figure 2.2)

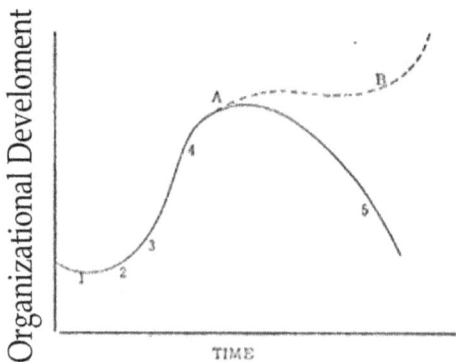

Figure 2.2 – Five stages of organizational development and growth

Stages of Organizational Development

The normal stages of organizational development are: (1) a weak association of individuals, (2) a formal organizational structure is established, (3) a period of maximum efficiency happens, (4) a more formal institutional stage becomes evident, and (5) disintegration of the founding principles and constructs leads to a decline in numbers or effectiveness, a redirection of programs and services, or death of the original vision.

These stages seem to suggest an ultimate demoralization of all organizations; however, if at the crisis point (A) which comes early in the institutional stage, creative initiative is brought to bear on the problems and the essentials of growth are properly supplied, expansion should continue until the growth curve (A-B) is repeated. The essentials of growth are: sufficient nutrients, energy in usable form, time, space, and the vitality of individual organisms. How does this translate to the present organization or institution? This is the real task of leadership.

Understanding the Thermostat

Understanding the thermostat on the wall could facilitate a grasp of the cybernetic process. The thermostat is a cybernetic process. It is a modern construct that demonstrates both the sympathetic or automatic changes triggered by the environment and the cybernetic or leadership role of establishing goals. A thermostat is designed to sense changes in the environment and activate controls that can make adjustments to the surroundings. This is akin to the function of a management and leadership team. Familiarity with this instrument on the wall may assist leadership in understanding how the system and the environment of the organization changes, how the people function in a changing society, and the leader's role in changing the conditions or atmosphere where they serve. Study diagram 2.3 below. It is a strong instructor for leadership.

Consider how the thermostat is perceived. When a worker continued to adjust the thermostat up and down they were asked to explain how the instrument worked. The answer, "On whatever temperature you set the thermostat, that's the temperature the air comes out." The answer was dazzling and demonstrated a total lack of understanding of the thermostat function.   My mother-in-law has an example of a different view. She thinks through the thermostat she can "hot shot" the heat and air conditioning system.   If the house is cold, she turns the temperature setting very high and says, "I hot shot it; it will get warm in a minute." She actually believes the furnace gets hot quicker the higher one sets the thermostat. The converse is true for her, the air conditioner works faster if one lowers the temperature setting to the lowest setting.   So much for conventional wisdom or the wisdom of old wives. Yet, some management and leadership teams seem to function in a similar manner.

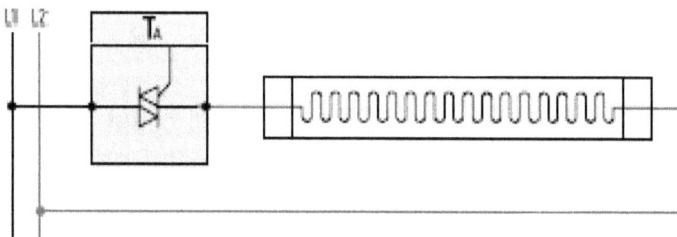

T_A = Ambient Temperature

Figure 2.3 - Input – Process – Output - Feedback Model of the thermostat

Leadership must be adequately informed about the science of cybernetics. Understanding the thermostat could be a benefit to both leader and people.   At least it would show an understanding for the lag time that is required to bring about change in an organization.   People do not perform just because the leader sets a high mark.   No matter how much one attempts to hot shot the system, it will move at the normal pace of social change. To push the envelope is to provoke conflict.

The Thermostat is a cybernetic system; by understanding the function and operation one can more clearly grasp the construct of sympathetic leadership cybernetics based on the Input-Process-Output-Feedback System.

1.   Input – the operator transmits desired setting;

2.   Process – the system determines how the HEAT/ AC should operate;

3.   Output – the cybernetic system of the thermostat measures the ambient temperature and sends a signal to the HEAT/AC system;

4.   Feedback – the temperature is measured and the system operates according to the pre-set level;

5.   Adjustment or Confirmation – after the feedback is analyzed the pre-set can be re-set to a different level by the operator or remain the same.

Application of the Cybernetic System to Leadership

1. Input could clearly be seen as a job description for   a member of staff.

2. Process is the communication of the expectation to the staff;

3. Output is the actual performance of staff;

4. Feedback is a positive or negative assessment of performance on which the leader makes a decision for correction or confirmation.

5. Adjustment or Confirmation – Negative feedback requires an adjustment or correction to a job description or staff behavior. This should be

done in private with the staff given opportunity to defend or explain.

6. Confirmation – Positive feedback deserves commendation or confirmation of a job well done and should be done in public.

Leaders should not attempt to manipulate the system. It is as foolish as one attempting to "hot shot" a thermostat. Leadership should exercise patience and work toward motivation rather than manipulation. It takes a little longer, but works with the system. Leaders who do not understand the difference do not last long or well serve the organization. A careful look at the Small Ball Theory (Figure 2.4) would provide a better view of the ills of pressing too hard for progress.

The Small Ball Theory

The small ball theory of leadership warns leaders and managers not to overdo the effort to motivate. Remember the subtle difference between manipulate and motivate: manipulate is getting others to behave in a way you want them to act; motivate is simply "motive" plus "action" and it suggests that leaders should understand the motive of others and provide a way for them to act for the benefit of both themselves and the organization. To confuse these two words is similar to over adjusting a thermostat. The small ball theory suggests that most managers misunderstand and overdo the effort to motivate. Motivation is in reality two words "motive" plus "action." Should the leader press the effort to motivate it could easily turn into manipulation.

Manipulation is getting someone to do what you want them to do for you, while motivation is a good understanding of what the individual wants (motive) and then providing a way for individuals to act (action) within the parameters of the organization to accomplish personal goals. When individuals

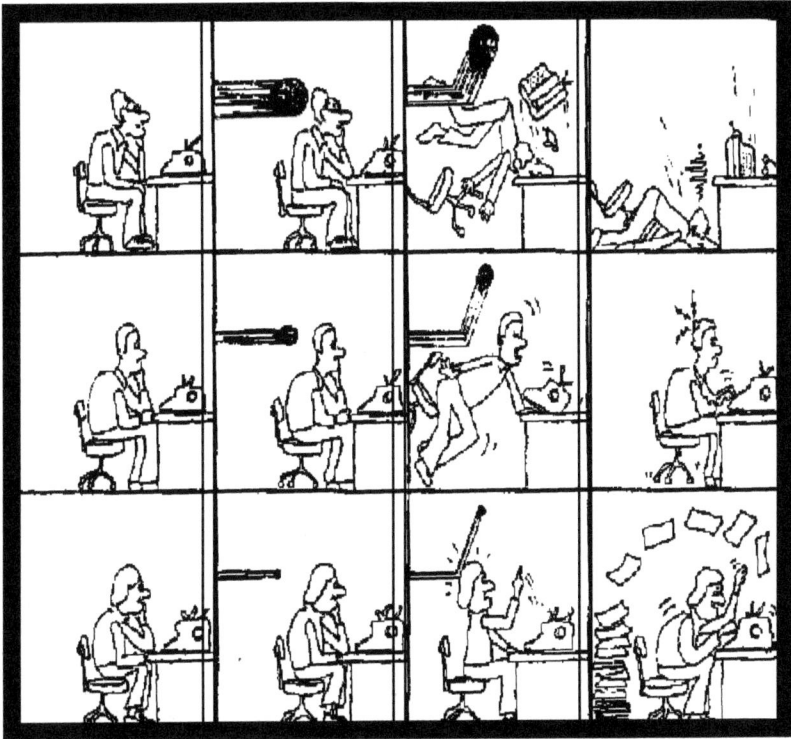

Figure 2.4 –The Small Ball Theory presentation.
Frame one: The ball was too large—no production. Frame Two: The ball was smaller, but still too large with little or no production. Frame Three –The right size ball will improve staff function and advance production

can accomplish personal goals and advance organizational objectives at the same time, cohesiveness (control) is established in an organization. This is a stable and desirable state for an organization.   When leaders understand the motives of people, they can provide the proper opportunity for action that will move the organization forward in the desired direction.

Leadership and Patience

Leadership must demonstrate patience, a word that St. Paul probably learned from Luke, the Physician.   Patience is a medical word and means to "remain under pressure" of a difficulty until relief can be found. That is why the Greeks called those persons who visited a Physician, "patients." One can easily notice in a doctor's waiting room individuals who are making an effort to remain under the pressure of illness until they can see the doctor.

A good example of patience is a small boy who falls on a tricycle and skins his hand and knee, but doesn't make a sound until he gets within ear shot of Mama or Grandmother. Then he yells as if he were dying. That is an exercise in patience. Leaders must learn to exercise patience with the people with whom they serve.

Skills akin to parenting are required for a leader in a nonprofit organization. A good way to explain this act of patience in parenting comes from St. Paul's dealing with the Thessalonians. Paul demonstrates the loving nature of a nursing mother and the discipline of a loving father. Paul encouraged with information, comforted with a maternal heart, and guided as a good father. Whether he demonstrated treasuring as a mother or the discipline and education of a good father, Paul modeled proper leadership in both the informal aspects of his ministry and in his formal role as Apostle to the Gentiles. (1 Thessalonians 2:7, 11)

An attitude is a predisposition to act. Leaders are working with attitudes of a group, not the opinions of an individual. Leaders must constantly assess the maturity of a group or organization to determine appropriate behavior to influence individual attitude or predisposition. Normally, individuals are part of an organization because they want to participate. Once leadership understands the motivation that causes one to join or participate in the organization, an appropriate program or individual opportunity can be provided to permit the individuals, and the group of which they are a part, to function for the good of the organization and keep the organization moving forward.

Information Sharing Patterns

Patterns of information sharing have been tested; some work better than others. Communication is the passing of information from one person to another. If not clearly understood, it becomes much as the party game of "gossip." In gossip, one would start the message by saying something like, "A green elephant stepped on a pink mouse." By the time it passed through a few ears and mouths it often became something such as "A pink alligator stepped on a green turtle dove." The message to be communicated must begin clearly, be transferred precisely, and interpreted correctly. There is always "static in the channel of communication." Leadership must carefully choose the pattern that best suits the circumstance, the message, and the organization. Most have heard the message between the college student and his father. Student sent a short message: "no mon, no fun, your son!" The reply was equally brief: "Too bad, so sad, your dad!" Normally individuals speak to and hear only those persons with whom they are closely associated. Study the patterns below to decide the best way to pass information in your organization.

Study and Review Questions for Chapter Two

1. How does the S-curve of growth related to all organisms and organizations?

2. Discuss the logarithmic or maximum efficiency stage of organizational growth.

3. Discuss the crisis point in organizational development.

4. How does a thermostat function as a cybernetic process?

5. What do you know about the Input-Process-Output-Feedback model?

6. Why should negative feedback be handled in private with staff?

7. How does manipulate and motivate differ?

8. How does the small ball theory related to a leader's patience?

9. Describe the best model for information sharing.

CHAPTER THREE

Situational Dynamic Relationships

A great deal has been written on the concept of leadership and until recently the main thrust of leadership has been defined by "characteristic traits." The resulting list looked strangely like a fitness report that could easily have been written for John Wayne in any number of his military roles. The disquieting feeling in the stomach that lingered after such a presentation was usually well-founded in the realization that there were certainly a lot of holes in this "traits list" when matching it to one's own traits. There had to be a better way to look at leadership and management.

More recent management and leadership theories have expanded through functional leadership in which leadership tasks are analyzed and understood in terms of situational and dynamic relationships. Several theories exist that describe a broad range of leadership methods on a continuum from authoritarian to participative behavior. These models present at least four contingencies: time, attitude, task, and relationship. The Tennenbaum--Schmidt Continuum of Leader Behavior. (Figure 3.1) suggests that TIME is a valid contingency.

Some words in Figure 3.1 should be changed to make them relevant to present day leadership. This is not just being politically correct, it is dealing with the affective domain of leadership, and the way people feel about leaders and the organizations of which they are a part. How and why would you change the following words: Boss, subordinate?

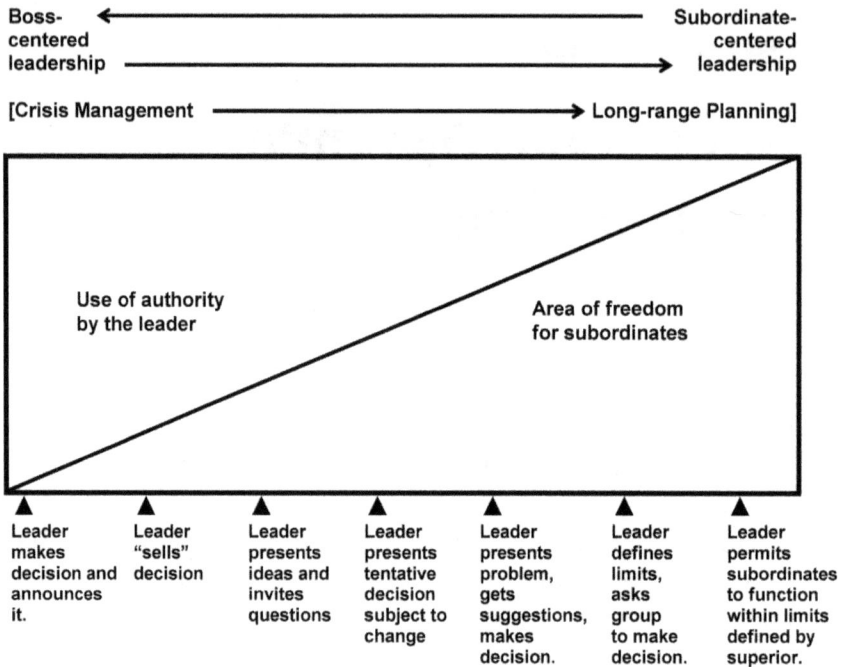

Boss-centered leadership ⟵—————————————————— Subordinate-centered leadership ——————————————————⟶

[Crisis Management ————————————————⟶ Long-range Planning]

Use of authority by the leader	Area of freedom for subordinates

| Leader makes decision and announces it. | Leader "sells" decision | Leader presents ideas and invites questions | Leader presents tentative decision subject to change | Leader presents problem, gets suggestions, makes decision. | Leader defines limits, asks group to make decision. | Leader permits subordinates to function within limits defined by superior. |

Figure 3.1—Tannenbaum – Schmidt Continuum of Leader Behavior deals with TIME.

Where would you place the contingency of "time" on the above Figure 3.1? By adding an additional continuum—"time" (meaning time available for the decision-making processes)— it becomes obvious that given little time, the leader is forced into making authoritarian-type decisions. This may explain the degree of crisis management that appears rampant in organizations.

Tannenbaum and Schmidt summarized their basic thesis in an article "How to Choose a Leadership pattern" as follows: (1) the successful leader is one who is keenly aware of those forces which are most relevant to the leader's behavior at any given time. The leader accurately understands personal limitations, the individuals and group being led, and the company and broader social environment in which the group operates. And certainly the leader is able to assess the present readiness for growth of colleagues.

This sensitivity or understanding is not enough, which brings us to a second implication. (2) The successful leader is one who is able to behave appropriately in the light of these perceptions. If direction is in order, he/she is able to direct; if considerable participative freedom is called for, he/she is able to provide such freedom. Thus, the successful manager can be primarily characterized neither as a strong leader nor as a permissive one. Rather, one who maintains a high batting average in accurately assessing the forces that determine what should be the most appropriate behavior at any given time and in actually being able to behave accordingly. Being both insightful and flexible, one is less likely to see the problems of leadership as a dilemma.

If this thesis is accepted, then the basic task of leaders becomes one of: (1) choosing the right leadership pattern for oneself, (2) knowing when to change it to another behavior, (3) considering the inherent degree of power and authority of the leader within the group, and (4) determining whether or not it is worth the time and effort to create the atmosphere for group advancement. The biggest mistake a leader can make is in being authoritarian when the situation is not appropriate and in not being authoritarian when it is appropriate. In any case, the leader must utilize those leadership behaviors which will produce the best results for a particular situation after considering task completion, individual and organizational needs, and desirability of group development.

Further leadership research into the related aspects of sociology and psychology produced some interesting efforts in the field of management. The leader's attitude seemed to make a difference. Douglas McGregor's "Theory X and Theory Y" introduced leadership attitudes into the practice of leadership. The "Theory X and Theory Y" idea proposed the idea that the leader's attitude should be based on the behavior of the group which could range from "Theory X": the worker is inherently lazy and doesn't want to work and therefore had to be coerced, to "Theory Y" wherein the worker likes to work and left to his own devices will grow and participate. Reality demands a "Theory Z", where the leader has an overall positive attitude. (Figure 3.2)   The second contingency is ATTITUDE.

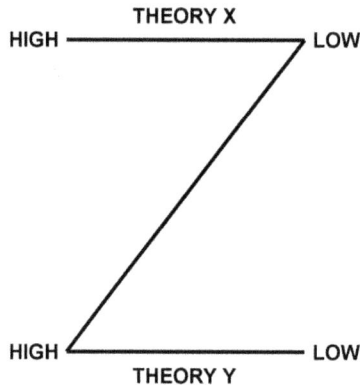

Figure 3.2– Theory Z represents a positive overall attitude of the leader who expects a low number of workers in the lazy category and high number of workers in the desiring to work category.

Others, notably Blake and Mouton, joined in the rejection of the "trait theory" and added the concept of attitudinal leadership constructing a grid using task (Concern for Production) on the horizontal axis and relationship (Concern for People) on the vertical axis, (Figure 3.3). When studying the figure, note the various contingencies in the behavior of the person in charge. One cannot choose a particular leadership style and use the same behavior in each situation. Circumstances change and so must the leader's behavior. To do otherwise, is to invite preventable difficulties in the operation of an organization.

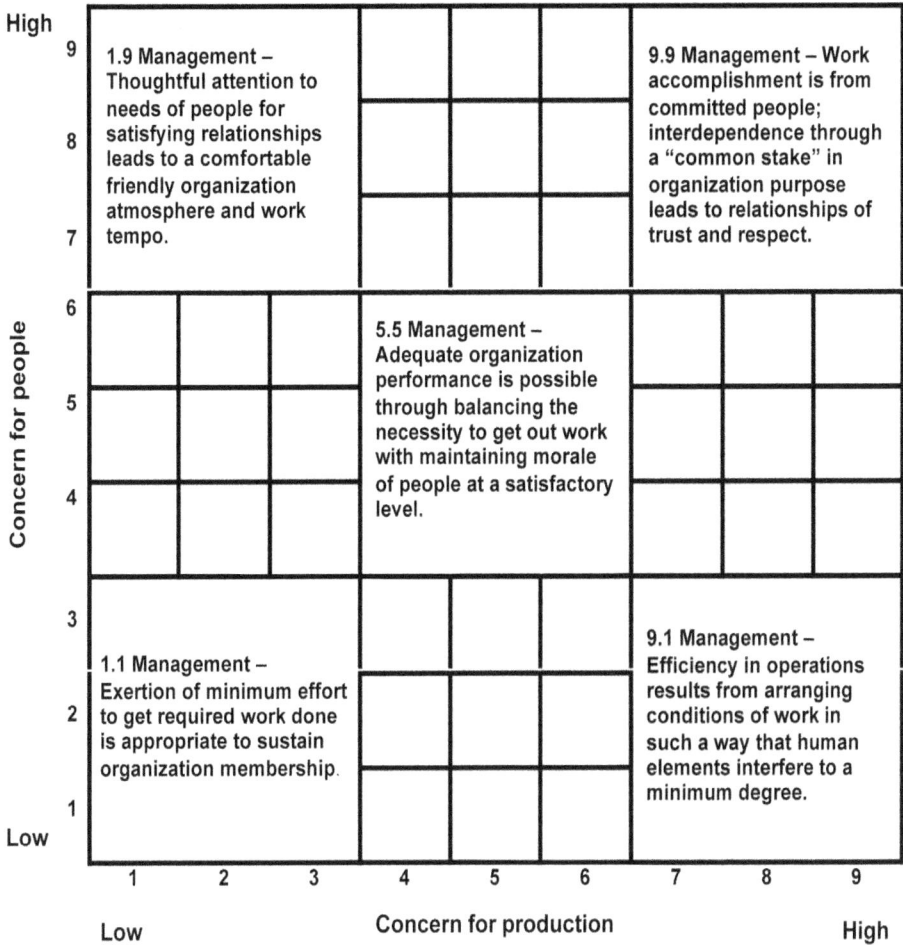

Figure 3.3 – Continuum of Leader Behavior

Certain questions must be answered before one could place themselves on the following grid (Figure 3.4). Usually the basic interrogatives provide sufficient data. Where am I? What day of the week is it? Who is with me? What time is it? How much time do I have to perform the tasks assigned to me? Who are the others involved in this task? Do I know the maturity level of the individuals or group? What should be my behavior at this time? The questions could continue, but at some point a decision must be made concerning the nature

High

9

8

7

6

Concern for people

5

4

3

2

1

Low

| | | | | | | | | |
| | | | | | | | | |

1   2   3   4   5   6   7   8   9

Low   Concern for production   High

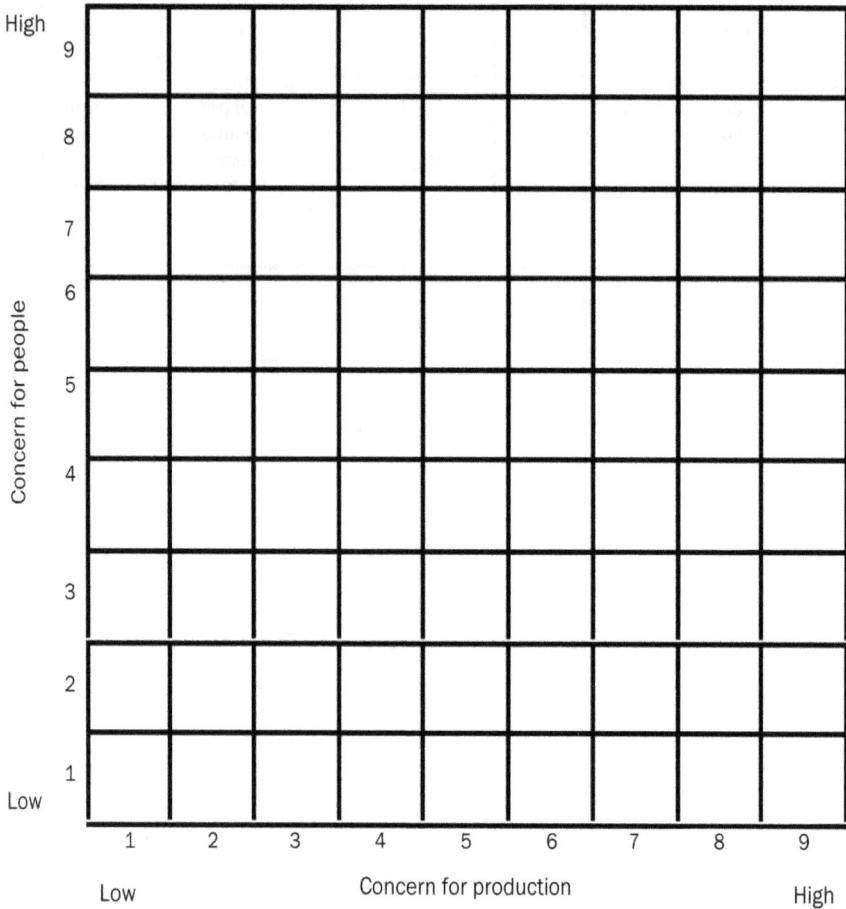

Figure 3.4--Place yourself on this grid.

of the response to both the task and the relationships. Each of the contingencies must be considered before the leader can behave properly under the circumstances. If the same meeting were held tomorrow with the same or different group, the leader's behavior may change. Why? The situation has changed. The maturity of the group has changed. The task has changed. The relationships have changed. These are the factors of contingency leadership, situational management or as some choose to identify as Life-cycle Leadership. Simply, it means that conditions change and behavior must change with these changing conditions.

The U.S. Navy did a good job in describing the changing behavior of leaders. They used the "N" man concept (Figures 3.5 and 3.6) to illustrate how one's role, function, task, relationship, and the circumstance necessitated the leader to alter attitudes toward the task and the relationships with the individuals for whom they were responsible. Naturally, some military tasks involve "win the battle, regardless of the cost in lives." Other personnel may see the whole battle differently depending on their leadership role and their relationship to

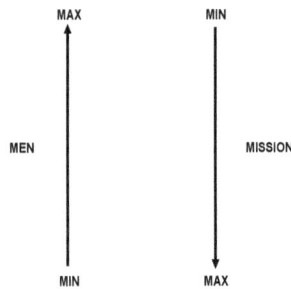

Figure 3.5-- By drawing the appropriate line describing the relationship between Men and Mission, i.e., the N-Man, high on relationship and high on task and so on through. H.ИU. P(π).N.

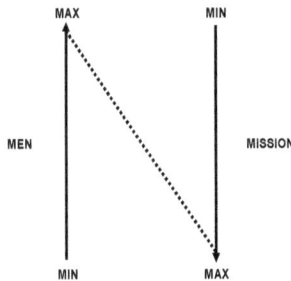

Figure 3.6–The N-Man, of course, is deemed the best and is regarded as the "ideal leader, i.e., John Wayne!

the task (mission) and the relationship (men) to the individuals participating in the battle

Another approach to the whole contingency theory is a model defined by Eric Berne, the founder of Transactional Analysis. It may be considered simplistic, but it does speak to the changes in attitude and behavior that confronts mangers and leaders constantly in organizational life. Human beings make up organizations and as humans communicate they open Pandora's Box of ills for both the leadership and the organization. An attitude being a predisposition to act that affects behavior under certain conditions or situations. A brief look at Transaction Analysis may demonstrate that this predisposition to act in a given manner is a valid contingency in leadership.

Berne's Transaction Analysis

Since interaction is key to adequacy in leadership it would behoove all interested in influence others to understand Berne's position in analyzing transactions between individuals. Berne's work is of value to the constructs of sympathetic leadership cybernetics because it is a simplification of the process of social intercourse and a method of analysis for studying interactions between individuals. His methods are simplified and used here to illustrate another way those involved in organizational activities can understand how and what happens and the natural forces that propels certain behavior in some circumstance. When an individual encounters another there is a transactional stimulus that requires a response. Berne related the response to the ego states behind each transaction. He believed there was a consistent affective pattern that stimulated the response behavior. Berne ultimately defined the three ego states as Parent, Adult, and Child. He described these concepts as phenomenological realities that are observable behaviors. This differs from Freud and others and Berne's definitions do not correspond to common English definitions of the words; however, it is assumed they are useful to the discussion of this text.

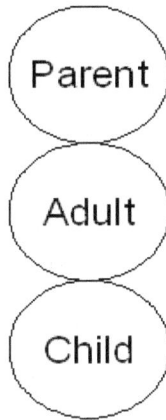

Figure 3.7 –The Parent relates to taught concepts; the Child deals with felt concepts; and the Adult utilizes learned concepts.

Berne's three ego states were the Parent, the Child, and the Adult. (1) Parent – Berne's parent represented a collection of external events experienced and recorded that influence one's perception of others in a given situation. Since a large part of this experience was imposed on the person during the early years from parents or others in a parent-like role this state was called "Parent." When Transactional Analysts refer to the Parent ego state as opposed to a biological or parent-like person, it is capitalized. The same is true for the terms Child and Adult. (2) Child – Berne's Child represented the record of internal emotions or feelings associated with perception of external events. (3) Adult – the Adult in Berne's model was the last ego state. A child begins to exhibit gross motor activity early in life and learns that certain situations can be controlled.   This experience initiates the Adult in a small child. The Adult grows out of the ability to see what is different when situations are observed or felt.

Berne described the Adult as being principally concerned with transforming stimuli into data, and processing the facts on the basis of personal experience. Others described the Adult as a data-processing unit that grinds out decisions after computing the data from three sources: the Parent, the Child, and the data which the adult has gathered and is in the process of gathering.

Practitioners of Berne's model use a structural diagram representing the whole personality of an individual and include the Parent, Adult, and Child ego states to construct a particular transaction.   The transaction in Figure 3.8 shows a Parent-Child transaction, with the Child ego state providing the transactional stimulus, and the Adult responding with the transactional response.

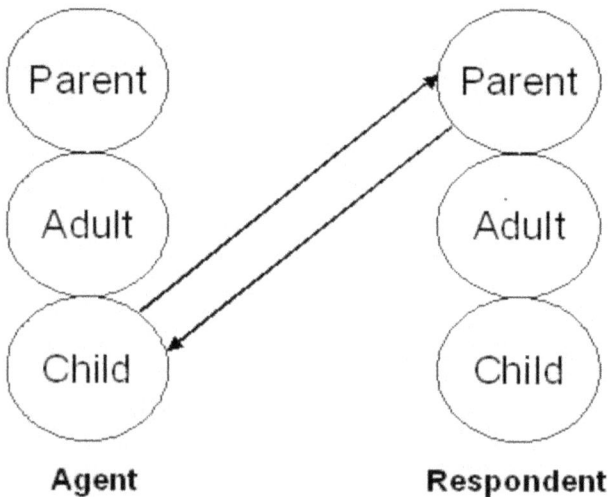

Agent   **Respondent**

Figure 3.8 – A complementary transaction.

The transactions above can be considered a complementary transactionsandisconsideredtobehealthyandnormalbecause there was no cross communication. Such communication may proceed as long as they remain complementary. The problem for leadership is that all transactions in organizations are not normal, healthy, or complementary. If the transaction is not normal it is considered a crossed transaction and can created real problems for managers and leaders. This happens when an ego state different than the ego state that received the stimuli is the one that responds. Figure 3.9 shows a typical crossed transaction when the Agent is an Adult and the Respondent is the Child. Such a transaction often occurs in intimate relationships such as marriage or long-term involvement in an organization.

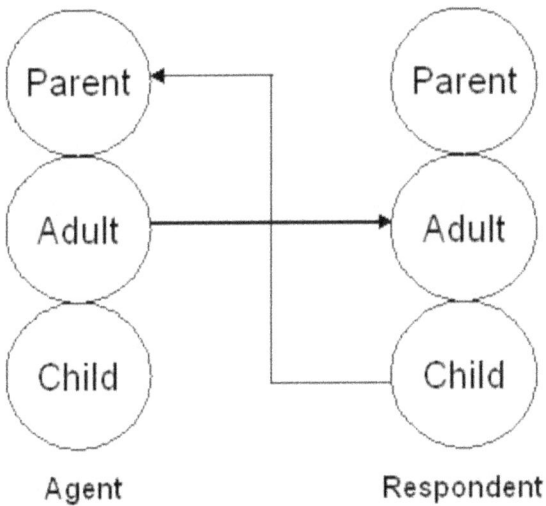

Figure 3.9 -- A crossed transaction

Those who manage and lead organizations may benefit from a clear understand of Berne's model of transaction. A major difficulty in organizational stability is in a failure to properly communicate one's true intentions or feelings to the group. Although an over simplification of the process it is clear that the baggage one brings to a relationship or to the functions of a group can create both good and bad times for all concerned.

Study and Review Questions for Chapter Three

1. Discuss functional leadership vs. character traits.

2. How and why would you change the words [boss} and [subordinate]?

3. Discuss the contingency of "time."

4. Identify the biggest mistake leaders can make.

5. How does the contingency of "attitude" affect behavior?

6. Relate "Theory Z" to "Theory X" and "Theory Y".

7. Discuss "task" and "relationship" as contingency factors.

8. How did the US Navy use the "N Man" concept?

9. How could you use the concepts in Transaction Analysis in your leadership role?

10. In I Timothy and Titus 1, Paul listed twenty (20) specific qualifications for leadership. Most of them are related to one's reputation, ethics, morality, temperament, habits, and spiritual or psychological maturity. Search these two chapters and identify the fundamental qualities of leadership. Make your own list using your own words. Remember, you are looking for qualities, not abilities, talents, or gifts.

CHAPTER FOUR

Stages of Maturity and Behavior

Contingency Theory and Leadership

Contingency or Life-cycle Leadership is an assumption about management and leadership that offers a choice of behaviors to a leader that produces the best chance of influencing others to get the job done. The contingency idea suggests location or situation. As a leader's situation or location changes so must the leader's behavior change. This assumption is a result of introducing leadership attitudes into the practice of leadership. Leadership is a complex problem, much like the search for the Holy Grail. The search and the research go on, seeking adequate leadership management assumption. The most practical and workable assumption of leadership is the life-cycle assumption. This is true because it is derived from actual everyday real-life experience.

Life-cycle Leadership is an assumption based on work done at Ohio University Center for Leadership Studies and the US Navy. It offers practical solutions to the basic problem of leadership behavior, based on given behavior of individuals and a certain level of group maturity. Hennesy and Blanchard expanded on this theory by providing a conceptual framework to enable leaders to recognize certain behavior within a group and choose a leadership style based on a combination of task and relationship that insured the probability of accomplishing a given task.

Contingency or leadership cybernetics   suggests that group development towards maturity has four stages, each requiring specific behavior modification by individuals within the group in order to achieve the most desirable stage which is Stage 4. (Figure 4.1)

The assumption also suggests that the leader must make behavior modifications as the group matures. The critical part is that the leader must know what behavior to exhibit concerning task and relationships whereas the group need not necessarily know or be aware of the changes in the leader's behavior.

A primary emphasis in the life-cycle assumption is on the behavior of the leader, but only in its relationship to that of his followers. The assumption is based on curvilinear association between leader task behavior and group relationships, and provides an insight into the relationship between adequate leadership and the level of followers' maturity. Followers are vital in any situation. They not only individually accept or reject the leader, but together they actually determine whatever personal power the leader may have in the group.

FORM	STORM	NORM	PERFORM
Why we are here	Bid for power	Constructive	Esprit de Corps
	COUNTER		
DEPENDENT	**DEPENDENT**	**INDEPENDENT**	**INTERDEPENDENT**
Mutual acceptance	Decision making	Motivation	Cohesive
	STAGE TWO	STAGE THREE	STAGE FOUR
STAGE ONE			
Immature			**Mature**

Figure 4.1 – Stages of Group Maturity

This is a multiple display [Figure 4.2] that deals with the leader's behavior in connection with the maturity of the group. Group maturity is shown in four stages: Telling, Selling,

Relationship

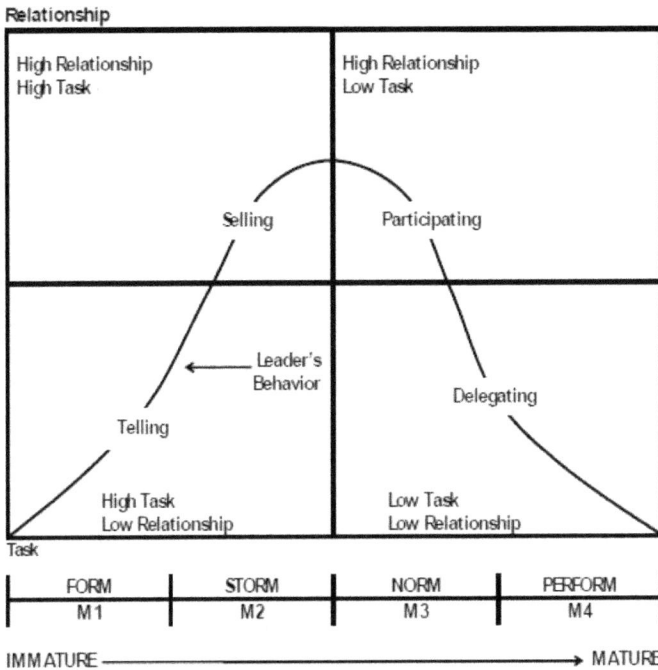

Figure 4.2– [M4]. The leader's behavior during each level is listed as [M1] Telling, [M2] Selling, [M3] Participating, and [M4] Delegating

Participating, and Delegating. The figure also shows the group maturity level as MI, M2, M3, and M4. A maturity continuum is shown and a task/relationship application to the leader's behavior.

The key to adequate leadership is the determination of group maturity. Recognition of the maturity level of the group is vital. The leader must exhibit behavior of that is appropriate to this maturity. The maturity level of individuals within the group is also crucial to leader attitude. The appropriate leader behavior may easily differ for an individual in a group than for the group as a whole.

Another way to view the cycle of relationship is to look at

marriage and the contractual-relationship that exists in this arrangement. Marriage seems to go through the same cycle as other contract relationships. See Figure 4.3. All contracts are a compromise. This is not a bad word: note com-promise; it simply means with promise. One agrees to

Individual and group response to the Task	"What's the task?" "Why am I here?" "Why are you here?" "I've got other things to do!"	Emotional response to task "I don't like it." "I like it." "Why do we do it this way?"	Roles defined Method of sharing resources worked out Work load divided and Coordination of work	Solutions to problems High efficient product Job done well with minimum effort
Relationship of individuals within the group	Testing, probing one another and leader Lessening the mistrust	Group checks leader's credibility if it doesn't like the task Polarization of group Cliques develop in groups Learning to trust others	Polarities and cliques dissolve Group begins to operate as a group Cliques and individuals begin to listen Begin to block out non-group members	Group energy focused on task Relationship taken care of automatically Relationship between members is supportive of each other and the task
Individual and Group Behavior	Mutual acceptance DEPENDENT	Decision making COUNTER DEPENDENT	Constructive INDEPENDENT	Cohesiveness/ Control INTER-DEPENDENT
STAGES	FORM Why we're here	STORM Bid for power	NORM Motivation	PERFORM Esprit de corps

IMMATURE...>MATURE

Figure 4.3– Life-cycle Leadership and Group Maturity

give up something to get something. This is life, and leaders must never forget that leadership of an organization is a true reality show. The phases or cycles are real and should be respected. When a leader understands the cycle or phase in which a group is operating, then the leader can stand firm without fear. It is the only way to survive in the organizational climate of the day.

Leaders must also note the data in Figures 4.3 and 4.4. There is a similarity to the data in Figure 4.5. A clear understanding of this data will arm a leader with the mental resources needed to be adequate in any position. It is clear in marriage

Model high	Allow emotional	Encourage	
Model high commitment to task.	Allow emotional response to the task to take place.	Encourage role selected by individuals.	Allow group to perform.
Set goals.	Identify the coalitions/ polarizations.	Encourage group consensus.	Encourage those things which prevent boredom.
State expectations			
Encourage disclosure of resources in relation to task.	Explain consequences and that they are unacceptable.	Roles may be different for short term focus than long, also for different environment.	Focus on environmental conditions which can be changed to produce more challenge.
Demand commitment and accountability.	Respond to credibility check honestly – don't punish.	Take advantage of opportunities.	Plan for the future.
	Negotiate an understanding or seek outside source to assist in moving block.		
	Maintain congruence and high concern for all members.		
High Task – Low Relationship	High Task – High Relationship	Low Task – High Relationship	Low Task – Low Relationship
MATURITY 1	MATURITY 2	MATURITY 3	MATURITY 4
FORM	STORM	NORM	PERFORM

Figure 4.4– Changes in Behavior of Leader

and group function that change in behavior is required to be equal to the present needs of either a partner or a group.

CYCLE OF RELATIONSHIP

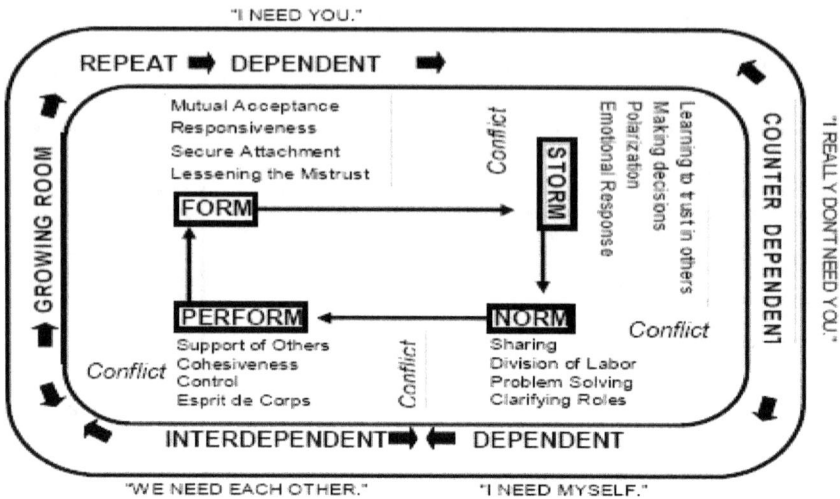

"I NEED YOU."

REPEAT ➡ DEPENDENT ➡

Mutual Acceptance
Responsiveness
Secure Attachment
Lessening the Mistrust

FORM ──────────────────➤ STORM

Conflict

Polarization
Making decisions
Learning to trust in others
Emotional Response

PERFORM ◄────────────── NORM

GROWING ROOM

Support of Others
Conflict Cohesiveness
Control
Esprit de Corps

Sharing
Division of Labor
Problem Solving
Clarifying Roles

Conflict

COUNTER DEPENDENT

"I REALLY DON'T NEED YOU."

INTERDEPENDENT ➡ ⬅ DEPENDENT

"WE NEED EACH OTHER."   "I NEED MYSELF."

- Conflict occurs between each phase. No gain without pain.
- Phases last from 1 to 5 years or extend until termination.
- Conflict resolution is required to proceed to the next phase

Figure 4.5—Cycle of Relationship

Probably the most universal application of the life-cycle assumption occurs in the parent-child relationship. The instinctive correctness of this assumption seems to be substantiated by this and other real-life illustrations.

Parent behavior changes overtime. If the parent uses only one style (i.e., high task and low relationship) in spite of maturity demonstrated by the child, it is quite probable that the child will remain either dependent or seek independence at the earliest opportunity. The high task/high relationship parent will wind up with a "mama's girl or boy," a child that does exactly what the parent wants. Even with age, the person remains immature and needing external direction and rewards and may never be able to "stand on his own two feet." Perhaps the "spoiled brat" emerge from the high relationship and low task parent?

The entire educational system is based on a growth development from high structure to little or not structure, from kindergarten to graduate work in which the structure or task is lessened and the relationship between teacher-leader and student-follower grows systematically less until the term for attending one of the acknowledged high seats of learning in the world, Oxford and Cambridge Universities, is described as "reading for degree or reading for examination." This implies external tasking and requires self-actualization on the part of the student with little, but valued, input from a tutor

The key to effective leadership becomes the determination of group maturity. Pfeiffer and Jones (Handbook of Structural Experiences for Human Relations Training, 1974) showed group development moving from Immaturity to Maturity through Movement from Stage 3 to Stage 4 Esprit-de corps and interdependent, requires unanimous agreement among members of the group. Groups will develop through these stages only as far as the members are willing to grow because each step requires personally giving up something of one's individuality for the good of the group. For instance, a move from Stage 1 to Stage 2 requires the membership to put aside discussion of the purpose and adopt a group purpose with which he or she may not completely agree. Further, the risk of personal attacks is greater when the issues become more meaningful.

In fact, a leader who manages always to be in the "right" place on the leadership line in relationship to the work group will be perceived by that work group as being High task/High relationship. Perhaps this ties together with the Blake, Mouton 9.9 person, the Navy N-Man, and the John Wayne character traits since the perception of the leader in the right place is that of the outstanding leader even though the leader may be in reality behaving in terms of low task/low relationship.

Leadership based on Life-Cycle constructs proposes that the leader's behavior should move systematically through four stages Quad 1, high task – low relationship; Quad II, high task – high relationship; Quad III, low task – high relationship; and Quad IV, low task – low relationship, which coincide with the movement of the group through the four developmental stages previously described. Since changes take place during the life-cycle of the group, leadership hinges so completely on the interaction of task and relationship, a clear understanding of these two terms is essential; Hersey and Blanchard offered the following definitions:

Task Behavior -- the extent to which a leader is likely to organize and define the roles of the members of a group (followers); to explain what activities each are to do and when, where, and how tasks are to be accomplished, characterized by endeavoring to establish well-defined patterns of organization, channels of communication, and ways of getting jobs accomplished.

Relationship Behavior – the extent to which a leader is likely to maintain personal relationships between himself/herself and the members of his group (followers) by opening up channels of communications, delegating responsibility, giving subordinates an opportunity to use their potential; characterized by socio-emotional support, friendship, and mutual trust.

The behavior of the leader then becomes, expressed in the simplest terms, akin to choosing a meal in a Chinese restaurant: complementary dishes from Column A and Column B (Task and Relationship). Depending on the observed and anticipated behavior of the group, the four basic leadership styles can be used effectively in order to get the best possible output regardless of which stage of formation the group is in. Appropriate behavior is described in terms of task and relationship for each stage of maturity. The leader models the Quad behavior appropriate for the maturity level of the group.

Understanding Power in Organizations

All organizations need to be analyzed in terms of power resources. According to Hardy (1986) useful taxonomies of power would be:

1. Positional or legitimate power, achieved by virtue of the position held;

2. Expert power, achieved by one's undisputed expertise or indispensability;

3. Personal or referent power, achieved through popularity or charisma;

4. Resource power, based on the capacity to reward or punish by giving or withholding resources;

5. Physical power, based upon the ability to coerce others.

6. Power in this sense is the ability to cause others to act in ways they would not otherwise choose to act by virtue of one's position, expert knowledge, popularity, resources or threats, according to the sources of power held. Each source of power is manifested through distinctive methods, used to obtain appropriate actions or patters of behavior.

7. Those with positional or legitimate power are able to exercise personal influence through the manipulation of rules and bureaucratic procedures, which are accepted because of the authority of the powder holder's position in the bureaucratic system.

8. Resource power is exercised through exchange processes, whereby the power holder offers resources in exchange for compliance with certain wishes.

9. Expert power is exercised similarly, so that the power holder provides expertise or information in return for compliance. Persuasion can also be used by those with expert power, and is the method commonly associated with personal power.

10. Physical power is demonstrated through the threat or exercise of force.

Such analyses enable those with planning responsibilities to assess both the sources of power held by individuals and groups influential within organizations and the methods by which they are likely to exercise that power.   Assessment can then be made of the possible outcomes of current and/ or potential conflicts, and of the strength and direction of such trends. Administrators can then examine the likelihood that particular plans will be supported or resisted by those individuals and groups, in pursuit of either overt or covert objectives.

The administrative/leadership process thus becomes the "art of the possible" - the assessment of strategies and tactics which will win sufficient support to succeed.   This involves the analysis not only of the potential resistance of identified individuals, but the possible coalitions that might form to resist the implementation of a plan.

Leadership goes further, then, by looking for ways to win over potential opponents and to weaken or prevent the formation of such coalitions.   Leadership depends on many things. Ones background and experiences plus time, task, attitude, maturity of the group and the willingness of the leader to change behavior as the maturity of the group changes. See Figure 4.6.

A chief difficulty in leadership is that normally everyone who is elected, appointed, or volunteered to serve in a given

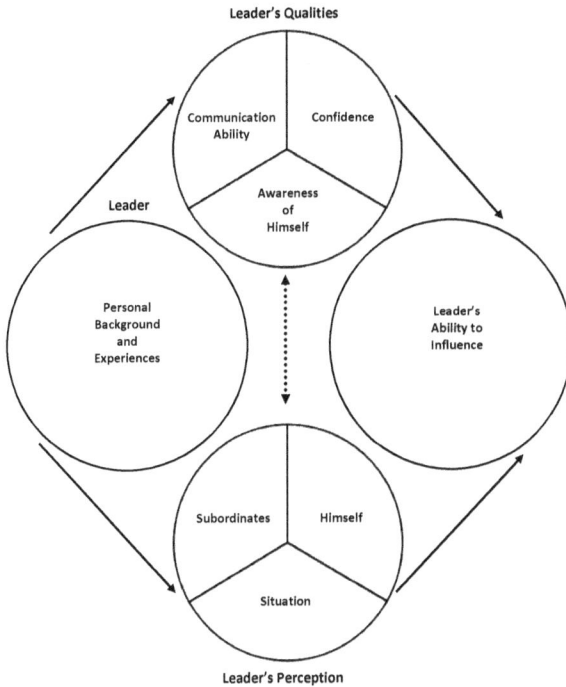

Figure 4.6–
Would you change any of the words in this diagram?

position is classified as a leader. Calling everyone a leader is to weaken the true function of leadership and to complicate the task of administration and management. Those who have positions have positional influence, but are not considered leaders unless they also have personal influence; that is, the ability to influence others to follow them voluntarily toward stated objectives.

To call individuals who simply hold a position a "leader" is to discredit the people who actually influence a group to accomplish the tasks assigned to them. In fact, when elected individuals perceive themselves to be in a leadership position, but do not understand the difference in positional authority and personal influence; such people will function in a manner that normally will alienate them from the group.

Role conflict comes in various forms. When a person has one understanding of a positional role, but others see the role in a different light, there is conflict. When others expect certain acts or performance from a position, but the person occupying that position does not clearly see that performance as part of their "job description" there is conflict. Whether it is personal-role conflict, inter-role conflict, or intra-role conflict, it is conflict, and this hinders the progress of any organization

It might assist the understanding of leadership for one to know that often leaders are not elected, appointed or in other ways named to a positional role; they simply assume the role of leadership because they have personal influence. A person in position must understand and utilize this influence for the advancement of the organization. Otherwise, it becomes a competition for position and power and that will destroy any organization.

The A's of Leadership
When knowing "how" is placed together with a "can do" attitude and this is coupled with experience and commitment to the task, the four A's of leadership are normally present to accomplish a task: attitude, availability, ability, and action. Availability means easy access at the point and time of need, while willingness demands a volunteer spirit, a dash of enthusiasm and teamwork. Leadership requires an ability to do and the availability to act plus a willingness to do or participate in the process. Ability is based on experience, expertise and knowledge appropriate to the action required. A good leader adds to this mix confidence and commitment to the task at hand to produce a readiness for action at several levels. See Figure 4.7.

Attitude	Availability	Ability	Action
A POSITIVE PREDISPOSITION TO ACT FOR THE GOOD OF ALL CONCERNED	READY ACCESS AT THE TIME AND POINT OF NEED	A CAPABILITY BASED ON PAST EXPERIENCE AND EXPERTISE	TIMELY ENGAGEMENT AS PART OF A TEAM
Priority One	**Priority Two**	**Priority Three**	**Priority Four**

Figure 4.7 The A's of Leadership

Characteristics of Leadership

Normally a leader displays over time four basic characteristics. This distinctiveness is expressed in both character and personality. The four qualities that make a leader recognizable are foresight, honesty, determination and audacity. (1) Foresight is witnessed in a leader's vision, creative ideas, and the ability to visualize a completed project or plan. (2) A sense of honesty validates leadership and is expressed in honest dealings, reliability, steadfastness and adherence to high moral principles. (3) A most convincing attribute of a leader is determination that includes a firm resolve, determination to remain steady over a long period despite difficulties or setbacks. (4) A true leader demonstrates audacity or courage with a fearless attitude and a willingness to challenge assumptions that may hold a group back from progress. This may be seen as bravery and boldness to speak a clear vision about the future.

Study and Review Questions for Chapter Four

1. Discuss contingency or life cycle leadership.

2. Identify the four stages of group development that affect leadership behavior.

3. Discuss why a leader's behavior varies from telling, selling, participating, and delegating.

4. How does FORM, STORM, NORM, PERFORM relate to task and relationship?

5. Discuss effective leadership and group maturity.

6. Explain task behavior and relationship behavior.

7. Describe power in organizations.

8. Discuss the interaction of leadership qualities and leadership perspectives.

9. From your own knowledge and experience discuss the reasons why organizational problems are never permanently solved.

CHAPTER FIVE

Shepherd Management

Shepherds and/or Fences

Some years ago traveling by train from London to Birmingham, England, many sheep were along the track. My knowledge of sheep was limited to the facts in the Bible. The only thing known was that sheep needed a shepherd. Seeing many sheep, but no shepherds, an English traveling companion was asked, "Are the shepherds on strike?" The answer was firm and clear: "We don't have shepherds; we have fences." With this knowledge, my understanding of sheep was expanded. Sheep must have either a shepherd or a fence and sometimes both are needed.

Metaphors about sheep and shepherding were used to illustrate the shortcomings of people in ancient writings. Leaders were called good and bad shepherds. "All we like sheep have gone astray" is a well known Bible phrase. Sheep received more attention in the Bible than any other animal and were important in the domestic, civil, and religious life of the people. As early as Genesis 4:2 sheep were mentioned when Abel was identified as a "keeper of sheep." Shepherd then was an early occupation.

Sheep and Shepherding

Previous generations who lived close to the land clearly understood the nature of both sheep and shepherding. Throughout Israel's history shepherding was respected. Shepherds in the field were the first to acknowledge the birth of Jesus; notwithstanding this honor, shepherds were despised by the orthodox Jews. Shepherds were unable to keep the details of the ceremonial Assumption; such as, meticulous hand-washing, because of their work. Being in the field constantly, shepherds were too busy to observe many customs and regulations. This busyness was probably the reason for the problem and should be a warning to busy leaders or managers today. The many management and leadership tasks may also create overworked individuals and prejudicial attitudes by others who do not fully and clearly comprehend the workload of Shepherd Management.

The Task of Shepherding

The Biblical sheep keeper was well prepared for the task of shepherding. As a protector, the shepherd carried a sling for defense against wild animals. A rod and staff were carried for counting sheep, support and use as a weapon (later the rod became a symbol of authority), and a flute for personal amusement and to bring contentment to the sheep.

Shepherds and the Sheepfold

The daily care and feeding of the sheep and their safety during the night were the primary responsibilities of a shepherd for the entire sheepfold. The shepherd was not the owner of the sheep, but was hired to perform a service. Sheep were considered passive and in need of positive guidance. It has been said that sheep will simply follow the feet in front of them without conscious awareness of danger or without regard to where they are going. It is this passivity and gullibility that require a shepherd or a fence to protect sheep from their natural disposition.

The shepherding herdsman guarded the flock against external enemies, tended to every need of the sheepfold, and guided the flock in a planned direction. Shepherds knew the quality of the pasturage and when to move to another location. Sheep were watered each noon and knowledge of the location of wells and streams became essential to shepherding. Watering places became important meeting places for shepherds or even whole tribes. Continuous care of the sheep assisted the shepherd to know each individual sheep by name and the shepherd's voice was known by the sheep. Sheep were always led, never driven. Since the Bible speaks of people in groups needing a leader, both shepherding and boundary markers are required to make church-related organizations work effectively and efficiently. This is a major function of Shepherd Management.

Shepherds and Bell Sheep

Jesus Himself was called the Good Shepherd and church leaders are often characterized as under Shepherds. The background of both sheep and shepherd informs the qualities and tasks of leadership and management today. As the manager gives attention to the sheepfold in general and individual sheep in particular, he/she is modeling the old shepherd of yesteryear. As an official of an organization, the Shepherd Manager guides, leads, directs, and advises employees and staff in the course of fulfilling the institutional mission through objectives, goals and standards.

Bell sheep are also a factor in understanding leadership. As a shepherd learns the characteristics and traits of each sheep, one or more are picked and given "bells" at the collar. These bell sheep have demonstrated that they follow the shepherd, obey commands, and are natural born leaders. The shepherd uses these bell sheep as part of the strategy to lead the sheep into green pastures.

Shepherd Management

Management is a function of an elected or appointed official in an organization. The person filling such a position is considered an officer. It is the executive function of planning, organizing, coordinating, directing, controlling and supervising any project, program or group with accountability for results. Since leadership involves influence, an officer must have influence beyond positional power to be classified as a Shepherd. The function of a shepherd manager is to serve the needs of the whole group without harming the individuals within the group.

The shepherd maintains maximum concern for and focuses on the collective operation of the group. As an officer, the Shepherd Manager exercises positional authority, but must also have personal influence to enable the group to function adequately. The shepherd quality is "truth" because individuals with authority must stand up for principle and morality and exercise positional power with courage to confront evil that would harm the organization. Since one rotten apple could spoil the whole barrel, the shepherd leader must demonstrate care and concern for the sheepfold and remove the bad sheep before it can damage the others.

In addition to good "bell" sheep that assist in leading other sheep in the right direction, there are likewise "bad" sheep in the fold. With apology for mixing a metaphor, but the best illustration to explain how the same kind of action can be both good and bad relates to fishing.

In Luke's Gospel (5:10), Jesus told Peter that in the future he would "catch" men. The word in the Greek is to "catch alive" and is used in 2 Timothy 2:26 to explain that men could be recovered from Satan's snare even though they had been taken "captive" to do Satan's will. In both cases the word indicates that one was "caught alive" to be useful for either good or evil. It is so in most organizations. In a normal distribution there will be good and evil; however, spiritual leadership must deal with both and attempt to make them productive for the welfare of all. Whether it is a shepherd caring for the sheepfold or a servant watching after a household, leadership has the common characteristic of influence.

Growth of an organization, although desired, may create unexpected difficulties. Organizational growth may produce a problem within the leadership team or in the general constituency. From this writer's perspective, there may be at least four areas where growth may create conflict. When the growth is a result of creative ideas by the leader, jealousy may develop within the team members or misunderstanding from the constituency. Should organizational growth come from the direction of a strong leader, the constituency may also become dependent on the leader for many other decisions, thereby losing creative ideas from the constituency. If growth were the result of the leader delegating responsibility to others without accountability, the leadership team could lose control of some aspects of the organization. A formal leader may enhance personal credibility and avoid some of the difficulties of growth by acting as a counselor/consultant within the formal framework of the organization. In this regard, the leader is seen as utilizing the legitimate authority normally attributed to a chosen leader.

Study and Review Questions for Chapter Five

1   What do you know about sheep?

2   Discuss the task of a shepherd.

3   Relate the "bell sheep" concept to leadership?

4   Examine shepherd management.

5   Compare good sheep and bad sheep.

CHAPTER SIX

Servant Leadership

The Essence of Leadership

The ability to influence individuals to voluntarily follow one toward stated goals is the true nature of leadership. When a leader can serve individuals and consequently advance the general good of the organization without the use of positional authority, this is the best of Servant Leadership.

In scripture, servants were under authority and responsible to and for others in the household. Servants worked and performed domestic chores, provided goods and services for the house, placed food before the family, and gave proper respect to the Head of the family unit. A manager serving as a shepherd may be concerned with external forces that may damage the group, but the servant, as a domestic, was to serve the family and look after the internal affairs of the household.

Servants and the Household

In ancient times servants were assigned various duties related to the people and the household. They were primarily concerned daily with their duties relative to the individuals assigned to their charge. A servant's goal was to meet the needs of individuals in the household, but there was a secondary concern for the wellbeing of the whole family. Naturally, each servant had a stake in the prosperity of the household so they were constantly aware of doing things in an economical way. The word "economy" comes from the Greek, *oikonomia*, meaning "management of a household."

One servant was assigned to the education of children. This male servant was called a schoolmaster, but he was not a teacher. He was responsible for preparing children for their lessons and to see that they were attentive and followed the instructions of the teacher. When the Bible said, "The law was a schoolmaster that brought us to Christ" (Gal.3:24,25); it did not mean that the law was the teacher, but that the law was the disciplinary aspect of bringing the Jewish people forward to prepare for the coming Messiah
.

The lead Servant was normally responsible for the efficient operation of all the people in the house and was charged with avoiding waste. A large part of the task was dealing with individuals, both the servant staff and individual members of the family unit. To accomplish this primary task, the chief Servant needed the ability to influence others to follow both the stated objectives for the Household and the individual goals for each member of the family unit.

The Essential Aspect of Leadership

All who assume functional roles in organizations must maintain the essential aspect of leadership: influence. One should not define management simply as having positional authority or identify persons who function only through personal influence as leaders. The ability to influence others is required in any position of responsibility. Although a manager has positional authority, this power alone is not sufficient to create a climate conducive to achievement. All functional roles in a group or organization require the ability to influence others. Often a leader in a group or organization functions well without positional power because of an ability to influence others in a meaningful direction. Consequently a manager, in addition to positional authority, must also demonstrate personal influence which is the essential nature of leadership.

Most individuals are better suited for either a shepherd or servant role, but these roles cannot be entirely separated. Although the ultimate accountability is different, much of the same essential qualities must be present. At times the key leadership function requires a combination of both the servant and the shepherd mindset. Although most individuals are better suited for one role or the other; individuals in top positions must have the characteristics of both a servant and a shepherd. Notwithstanding this duality, a manager must remember that their primary concern is the organization itself. Also, individuals in a place of influence must not only be concerned with individuals, they must have an overriding concern for the total welfare of the organization

King David was a scriptural example of the perfect combination of shepherd and servant qualities. He was a servant of God and a shepherd to the people. A strong passage dealing with false shepherds, Ezekiel 34:11-31, dealt with God as the True Shepherd and David as a key leader (vs. 23). "And I will set up one shepherd over them, and he shall feed them, even my servant David; he shall feed them, and he shall be their shepherd." It often requires a "god-like" quality to handle the duality of management and leadership. When this is not evident, both the organization and the individuals suffer greatly.

Human Aspiration

In the New Testament, Mark presents Jesus as both King of Kings and as a Servant. Following an example of carnal ambition, James and John sought position and wanted to be seated on the right hand and left hand of Christ. This human aspiration for authority in the Kingdom disturbed the other ten disciples. Jesus clearly made a distinction between the way some attempt to "rule" as lord over God's heritage and others who would demonstrate the humility of "servant" leadership.

> But Jesus called them to him, and saith unto them, Ye know that they which <u>are accounted to rule over the Gentiles exercise lordship over them;</u> and their <u>great ones exercise authority</u> upon them.

> But so shall it not be among you: but whosoever will be great among you, shall be your minister: And whosoever of you will be the chiefest, shall be servant of all. (Mark 10:42-44).

Many words and constructs of the past are less than adequate to inform management and leadership in the nonprofit sector. This book is about organizations and leaders today. Words and thought forms inherent in the terms used by organizations of past generations are misunderstood by an urban, complex world; such as, boss, executive, foreman, landlord, principal, chief, owner, superintendent, overseer, bishop, and particularly the use of the concept "subordinate." These words normally send negative messages to the people in contemporary organization. Although the words of scripture; such as, sheep, shepherd and servant are even more ancient than the institutionalized words mentioned before, yet, the inherent sense of these words have positive meanings and can assist present leadership in finding better words to describe their actions. The primary value is to assist in a change of perception that individuals work "for" someone; in reality in today's environment, individuals work "with" others. It is better to say "John works <u>with</u> me in management!" Than to say the usual, "John works <u>for</u> me in....." Consequently, the word subordinate meaning [lesser, minor, subsidiary, inferior, lower, secondary] can easily be changed to colleague meaning [a coworker, associate, partner, collaborator]. Changing some of these key words is required to fully understand ones function in areas of management and leadership in the nonprofit segment of organizational life.

Funds Available Budget

Nonprofits normally have a funds available budget and thus limited funds with which to fulfill their mission. This fact alone changes the whole character of management and leadership in the organization. Staff and employees must be more committed to a nonprofit. Most could work elsewhere and make more money, but they choose to work in the environment of a close knit organization where individuals depend on each other rather than on just cash flow. The attraction and retention elements of the nonprofits are stronger than the cash benefits of other work. The attitude of leaders and the workforce is positive. Everyone knows that everyone else is working because they want to be connected with an organization providing a product or service that can make a difference. There is usually a missionary mindset in an eleemosynary organization. Depending on donations, grants, fees or tuition requires both managers and leaders to have a clear understanding of the limitations placed on them by cash flow. This simply means that when funds are limited, influence (leadership) must be unlimited to keep the organization moving forward. Relationship building is a central task in a nonprofit organization.

Part of the difficulty in understanding leadership in a nonprofit enterprise relates to the intrinsic and extrinsic values held by members of the organization. Money is not the only commodity that attracts good people to an organization. What people know and feel about the organization must be factored into the equation. Whether an individual worker has a "volunteer mindset" or a "paid employee" mentality, must be considered. Most people believe that a good worker will not work for a bad company regardless of the pay. Likewise, the conventional wisdom is that a good worker with confidence in the mission, the people and the product/service of an organization, together with feeling comfortable in the work environment, may not be easily enticed away by money.

Volunteers vs. Hirelings

When key staff members are employed for a limited stipend they should be viewed as volunteers and not hirelings. A hireling is one that works solely for compensation. Scripture dealt with the problem of hirelings by declaring that a hireling would abandon the sheep if a wolf were in the vicinity. "The hireling fleeth, because he is a hireling, and careth not for the sheep." (John 10:13)

A volunteer's stipend is not a salary, but a strict and regular allowance provided to free the individual to pursue the work or chosen career. Granted it should be a living wage, but the stipend is based on a salary reduction agreement that reduces the compensation for services. Even the U.S. Government understands that nonprofits contract with professionals for less than the person would be paid at a for profit establishment. The IRS permits the nonprofit to "book as donated services" this difference. Most staff members see this agreement as a contribution to the ongoing mission of the organization.

The missionary wages provided by many nonprofits fit the original definition of the word "stipend." The word origin is from the Latin, *stipendium,* meaning "soldier's pay." With this in mind one should consider the volunteers working for nonprofits as "soldiers" for the cause and treat them with the same respect and honor that one attributes to the men and women serving in the all volunteer Military Service. Most everyone knows that soldiers are paid less than they would receive in civilian life. Yet, many volunteer to serve and remain in Military Service until retirement. It is not just those who cannot find a job that volunteer for Military Service. Some who volunteer for the wrong reasons self-select themselves out and find other employment. Others learn to live on the income available and see their work as an ongoing ministry to others. One lesson shared with me from a staff of a nonprofit was clear: "I have learned that no matter how much money I make the same amount is left at the end of the week, "nothing." This person had learned to live on the stipend provided and remained happy in the work of the organization.

This reminds me of a story about a young pastor who resigned to accept the call of a larger pastorate. A Deacon chided the young man that he was going to the other church simply because it had more money. To this the young man responded, "The love of money is the root of all evil. If they have more money, they have more evil, and they need me the worstist!" It is not the level of the pay, but the level of commitment to the mission, the cause, the end product of the organization that creates any atmosphere conductive to shepherd management and servant leadership.

Men and women with career goals, professional training and graduate education participate on a volunteer basis in the military and in other charitable and socially responsible assistance programs. Most of the nonprofit schools in America fall in this category and are served by volunteer professionals who choose to participate. Nonprofits do not "draft" individuals to work "for" them, individuals volunteer to work "with" others to advance a worthy institution and willingly donate a large portion of this service to advance the cause of the organization. This is the kind of men and women that have deep feelings for people and want to be in a service industry. These are the people that can change the world one person at a time.

Judgment Based on False Assumptions

When one does not understand the inner working of a nonprofit organization, they may be prone to make judgments based on false assumptions. For example, after observing the budget for faculty salaries, a conversation with an educational consultant included this exchange, "I believe you have set a new low for faculty compensation." The answer was firm and clear, "No, we have established a new high for faculty commitment!" It is this kind of commitment that is required to build and stabilize a nonprofit organization.

It is incumbent as a pressing obligation and duty, those personnel serving management and leadership in nonprofit positions be fully aware of the nature of the people they lead and with whom they work.   Unless upper level staff demonstrates a shepherd mindset and a true servant mentality, they are not worthy to lead such "soldiers" onto the spiritual battlefield that most nonprofit and/or religious organizations have a mission to serve.   People who serve nonprofit causes are especially gifted in both spirit and skill and generally are more effective and efficient than others who work just for a paycheck.

Educating Future Leaders

The task of educating future leaders in the context of a secular world, where ethics and values have little meaning, requires committed leadership.   Raising charity funds for inner city programs necessitates a clear understanding of the antecedent causes for the poverty and evil.   Growing a church congregation or operating a "rescue mission" in the midst of a carnal and sinful community calls for God called leadership. Leading volunteer "soldiers" into spiritual warfare demands both strong and courageous leaders who know by name and ability each individual following them into the daily conflict with the negative forces that initially created the need for their organization. As long as that need exists, the organization will need leaders with vision, courage, integrity, and perseverance. Ongoing commitment is required to provide a nonprofit perspective of leadership and management relevant to the Twenty-first Century.   Such organizations cannot function with officials using only positional authority; there must be an ability to exercise personal influence which is the sense of leadership.

Positional Authority vs. Personal Influence

To operationally define the concept and the constructs of leadership, one must understand both the formal positional authority of an "officer" and the informal personal influence of a "leader."   Leadership is essentially the ability to influence and/or persuade individuals to follow the leader voluntarily toward the stated goals of the organization. This facilitates a culture of growth, development, and harmony in an organization and creates an atmosphere conducive to both shepherd management and servant leadership.   One weakness in most organizations is that these two constructs are not adequately utilized.

Servant Leadership

The practice of serving the needs of individuals in the context of a group or organization to accomplish established and understood objectives is Servant Leadership.   This kind of leader focuses on serving the welfare of individuals for the benefit of the organization, while managers are concerned first with the welfare of the organization that consequently benefits the individuals.   The "servant" mindset centers on the individual to be served and the internal affairs of the organization, while the "shepherd" concentrates on the whole operation of the organization.   Although, the shepherd has concern for the people, the positional responsibility is primarily for the general good of the group or organization.

A Person of Influence

Servants extend care, but may only be a person of influence rather than an official or officer of the organization. A servant leads in humility (Philippians 2:3-5), with a Christ-like attitude. A servant leader has the quality of "grace" that enables the leader to act without regard to merit in treating everyone fairly and justly. The servant leader is a personal encourager, a good listener, supportive and friendly at all times. This makes the "servant" vulnerable to abuse and disrespect from some being served and requires that the organization provide certain protocols of respect that safeguard those willing to serve.

The servant primarily addresses individual needs in context of the group or organization, while the shepherd is concerned more with the collective need of the group and/or organization with individuals being the secondary beneficiary. Focus or emphasis seems to be the significant difference between a shepherd and a servant. One looks to the whole and then the part, while the other looks at the parts that make up the whole. Both require the ability to influence others to follow them toward stated objectives. Both are accountable to someone for the results or outcomes of their efforts. And each leader must demonstrate both knowledge and an understanding of the primary institutions ordained and ordered by God: the family, the community, and the church. Without a clear and objective view of these institutions, a leader will have difficulty understanding the people and the problems associated with the workforce of an organization.

Study and Review Questions for Chapter Six

1. What is the essence of leadership?

2. Discuss the meaning of economy?

3. Compare positional authority & personal influence.

4. Evaluate words of the past as they relate to leadership.

5. Indicate how leadership differs in a nonprofit and a for profit organization.

6. Discuss a funds available budget.

7. What is the origin of the word stipend?

8. What is servant leadership?

9. Discuss the focus of a shepherd vs. that of a servant.

10. From your own knowledge and experience, discuss the function of a manager as a leader rather than only an administrator or decision-maker.

CHAPTER SEVEN

Source of Inspirational Guidance

Divine Viewpoint

From the Divine viewpoint, the creation of mankind was good. According to Genesis, both man and woman were fashioned by the hands of God and placed in a sinless Paradise. Yet, in spite of divine patience, the first couple could not make this simple system work for the good of all. They messed up the Paradise and now all mankind functions in a complicated world filled with evil. Since an organization is made up of living human beings, one would expect difficulty with the human element in the workplace. All human beings suffer from a flawed nature and a blemished environment in a sinful world. This daily impacts the behavior of management and leadership in organizational life. As people change, the leader's behavior must adjust to the maturity level of those being led.

Three Basic Institutions

Understanding how human beings function in families, groups, and organizations is a precondition to creating an atmosphere conducive to progress and the prevention of failure in organizational life. A foundational philosophy of life begins with three basic institutions. These institutions were ordained and ordered by Divine Providence. First came the established family, followed by groups of families coming together into a constituted community with authority, and at last the followers of Jesus first worshiped in homes but soon these house churches became the organized church. These three: family, community, and church were the basic units that were divinely ordained and ordered to produce, protect, and preserve individuals. All institutions and organizations should be placed in these classifications to be clearly understood. For example, community authority includes government, the courts, business, education, and many other aspects of human life and development.

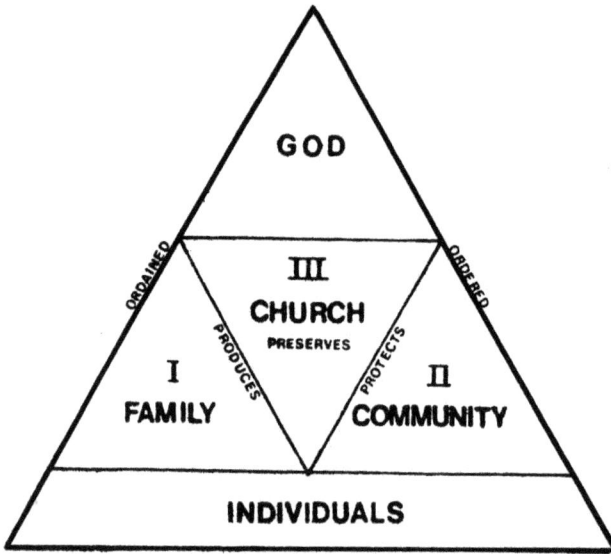

Figure 7.1 – Basic Institutions are related to the Individual. A Higher Power reaches the individual in the context of basic institutions. All institutions must work within these boundaries to be effective.

Management and leadership must clearly understand that the primary concern of Divinity was individual welfare. When concern for individual rights and justice is placed on the back burner in order to increase bottom line profits, evil is apparent in the process. In a nonprofit organization, an individual can never become just a number to be discarded or dealt with arbitrarily. Of course, there are times when behavior violates organizational culture and eliminates an individual from productive involvement in a particular organization. In such case, the leadership must function for the good of the whole.

Each institution was initiated for the good of the individual. These three fundamental institutions are interrelated and cannot survive alone. God ordered and ordained that individuals should be produced within an established father/ mother family, protected in a constituted community with authority, and preserved in the context of both family and community in a gathered and loving church fellowship.

The family produces individuals within a framework of Divine order and the established laws of society. When individuals are born without the care and nurture of a loving two-parent family, many problems are inflicted on the community as a whole. Some of these difficulties become evident in the life of organizations and institutions. Problems in the home are carried over into the community and the church. Leadership must function with a total awareness of this carry over. In fact, many of the problems in organizations are directly related to problems in personal and family life. At times, organizations also suffer from this carry over.

Managers and leaders in organizations can benefit from a study of living systems theory (LST). All societal professions, including medical, legal, educational, counseling, accounting, and religious, are directly and obviously concerned with three levels of living systems, i.e., organism, group, and organization. Less directly, but quite obviously, they are also concerned about the levels of community, society, and supranational systems. Therefore, by the nature of their concerns, the social professions are cross-level disciplines. LST provides a handy set of vocabulary, concepts, and postulates in a logical framework to facilitate research and understanding in the social disciplines.

Individuals are protected by constituted community authority. In this effort, the community even protects the guilty from the wrath of individuals. Yet, the community is structured to punish individuals who violate the conventional wisdom of community authority. Organizational life must consider both the protection of the individual and the separation of those individuals who would harm the community.

God ordained and ordered the organized church to preserve individuals within the family and the community. It is within the family that the church receives members and the community provides opportunity for service and outreach. The individual members of the church have a role in both functions.
Parents are to dwell together in harmony so their prayers will not be hindered. Partners in marriage are obligated to separate each other from participation in the evils of the community lest their children become defiled. Yet, each individual is responsible to God, the church, the community, and the family to conduct their life in keeping with stated moral and ethical standards. When these standards are broken, everyone suffers including the organizations and institutions in the community

Organisms, Groups, and Organizations

Management and leadership are concerned with the levels of organisms, groups, and organizations as they deal with the culture of the institution. As new people come into an existing operation, there is a time-lag in adjusting to the culture. Leadership must demonstrate patience during this adjustment period. Everyone needs time to modify their attitude and behavior to meet the culture of the group.

Organizational Socialization normally takes from 1 to 6 months. A new individual coming into an organization learns the rules of the organization and develops relationships with the people and the institutional culture during the first few months. This is also true of new individuals coming into the organization at the management level.

Individual Empathy for the institution at times takes up to 12 months. It is not easy to develop sympathy or compassion for the plight of individuals in an institution. The meaning of belonging to an organization and learning the expectations of peers and organization leaders is developed over time.

Management and leadership Autonomy is not normally reached during the first year of operation. It may take one full year for an individual to fit the concept of the organization and the institutional culture into a lifestyle of service and personal growth as a productive partner in a mutually rewarding enterprise.

Confidence is a Factor

Organizational growth and development begins with confidence. There must be confidence in the organization of which one is a part. Confidence in the product or service produced by the organization is required. There must also be confidence in the people with whom one works. Without confidence in these categories or operation, no organization can function properly regardless of the quality or quantity of management and leadership efforts.

Purpose, Objectives, Goals, and Standards

The purpose or mission of the organization is singular and directional. It provides a general direction toward the long-range reason the organization operates. Although singular, this purpose must be sub-divided into reachable and measurable objectives and goals. Objectives, goals, and standards are always plural, similar to parallel structure in sentence structure. Some may choose to use goals, objectives,

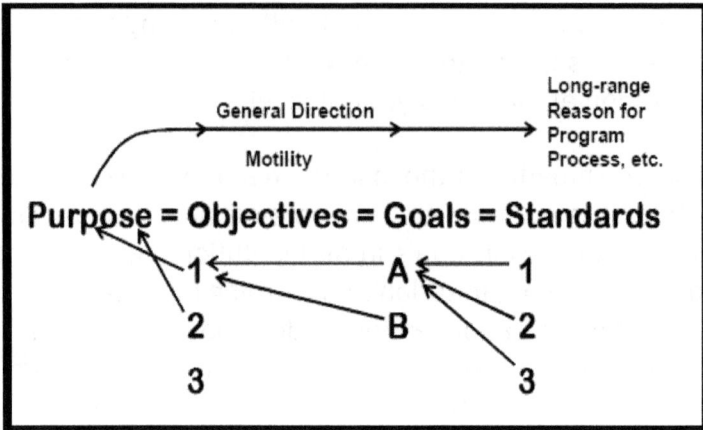

Figure 7.2– Purpose, Objectives, Goals, and Standards

aims, etc., but the rule follows: each must be a subset of the previous order. A purpose may be divided into two or more objectives. An objective is divided into two or more goals. If only one objective were determined, it would be a restatement of the purpose. Standards are criteria by which achievements are measured and must be multiple. This follows the same rule as an outline in writing: one cannot have a "1" without a "2" or an "A" without a "B", etc.

An objective is a specific aspect of the purpose; when accomplished, it advances the organization in the right direction. Goals are specific aspects of an objective; when reached, an objective is accomplished and the purpose is advanced. A standard is a measurement by which performance can be evaluated. Normally, there are three categories of standards: (1) performance, (2) efficiency, and (3) effectiveness. Performance is the ability to carry out, accomplish, function, and discharge a duty or deed. Efficiency is productivity without loss or waste. When effectiveness is measured, it demonstrates readiness for service or action and suggests adequacy or competency.

When management and leadership deal with the purpose or mission of an institution, direction is provided that guides action. Normally one is given direction only once, but may constantly need guidance along any journey. Consequently, one who leads must be guided by the purpose for which the institution was organized. The general competency of the workforce determines performance at specific competency levels. General performance is measured by the efficiency of reaching objectives and goals. The goals are milestones along the journey to measure progress and to provide encouragement. Should goals be divided into short-ranged and long-ranged goals? The long-ranged goals exist to prevent discouragement with short-ranged failures. There will be failures because all organizations consist of human beings. However, the setting of priorities improves efficiency and effectiveness.

Planning Process Determines Action

Motility results from action and is spontaneous use of power that moves the purpose in a forward direction. In order to achieve motility there must be purposeful action not just activity or busyness; there must be a planning process. When leaders are sure of where they are going and clear of what they are attempting to do, the best methods can be used to complete the process. When this is done adequately in a timely manner the process will achieve satisfactory results. This can only be done if the choice of methodology is a result of a planning process.

Three Reasons for Planning

There are three reasons for planning in organizational life. First, management and leadership must (1) plan for the future. Unless this is done one cannot fulfill the second reason for planning, which is to (2) take advantage of opportunities. When leadership understands the purpose, knows the objectives, values the goals, and is clear on the standards by which achievement will be measured, they can take advantage of each opportunity to advance the purpose. Only then should leadership take time to (3) deal with problems.

Contrary to popular belief, problem solving is not the main function of upper level executive leadership. Planning for the future and taking advantage of every opportunity to move forward is the priority. Problem solving is something best done on a "rainy day" when all the priority activities are in place. Many problems are solved through using the opportunities that circumstance presents. Usually, this is accomplished

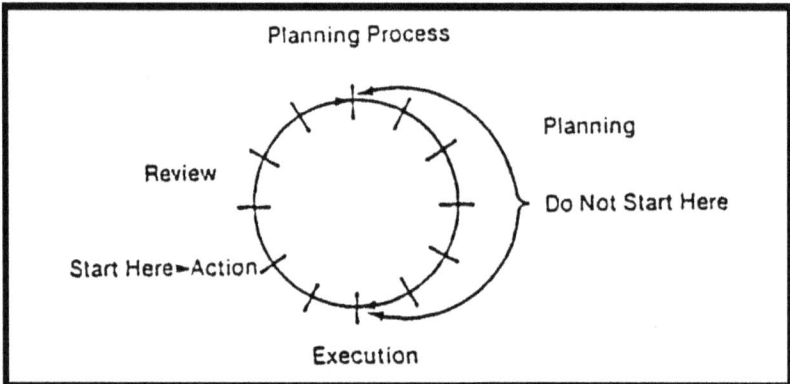

Figure 7.3- The planning process.

by asking three questions: What can be done better? What can be done differently? What can be done new? Of course, there are times when problem people become a priority of leadership, but the upper tier staff should never concentrate only on problems.

The Planning Process

Planning is a cycle and must be viewed as moving clockwise. From noon until 6:00 o'clock is "planning time," but half of the work is done before one reaches the "execution phase" at 6:00 o'clock. The emphasis is "Do not start yet, wait until the planning phase is completed." Although "execution" officially begins at 6:00 o'clock on the dial, "action" does not start until the planning clock reaches 8:00 o'clock. Then the "review process" begins simultaneously with the "action" and continues until 12:00 on the dial. Now, the process starts over. It is a continuous endeavor and includes three kinds of planning. (1) Planning for the future. (2) Planning for opportunities. (3) Planning to solve problems. The process must work in this order. Should one start with attempting to solve problems, the opportunities would pass and the future would overtake an unprepared organization. It should be remembered that planning time is productive time. The longer the planning time, the less time it takes to execute the plan and methods.

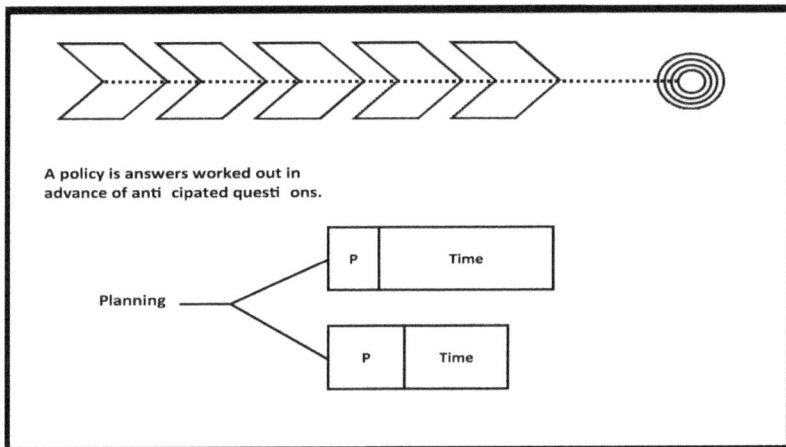

A policy is answers worked out in advance of anti cipated questi ons.

Planning

P | Time

P | Time

Figure 7.4. –
Planning lessens Time, Policy Guides Action

Only after leadership has used each opportunity to advance the mission of an organization in the direction of the purpose should time be given to solving problems. Before the planning cycle is restarted that deals with planning for the future, leadership must make corrections to the inferior process.

Once an analysis of difficulties is made, leadership can begin constructing a superior process to move the organization forward. This planning process will result in a revision of both policy. Policy is answers worked out in advance for anticipated questions. Methodology includes the approach one takes to answer all unanswered questions and the course of action required to move the organization toward the stated goals. Leadership must remember that one may not construct a superior process until the inferior process has been corrected. The proper order: correct the inferior before attempting to construct the superior.

Study and Review Questions for Chapter Seven

1. Identify the three basic institutions and their relationship to the individual.
2. Discuss the time-lag for new people entering an organization.
3. How is confidence a factor in an organization?
4. Analyze [purpose, objectives, goals, standards]
5. Compare motility and activities.
6. Enumerate the three reasons for planning.
7. How does policy and methodology relate?

CHAPTER EIGHT

Separate Strains of Thought and Process

Perspectives and Patterns

The relative fixed relationships that exist among people in an organization establish patterns of interaction and coordination of the technical and human elements of groups and/or organizations. This relative fixed relationship is known as structure. Analyzing human activity in the context of interaction between people is called process. When one observes the goal-directed activity of people in an organization, this is measurable behavior. This means that criteria or standards, such as job descriptions and production goals, must exist by which behavior is measured in relationship to the distance between the real and the ideal in the organizational climate, culture, and mission,- leaders must work within the structure, understanding and observing the process related to the interaction of people in the organization, and observing and measuring the behavior of the organization and the individuals involved in the ongoing operation of the enterprise. Managing all of this for the good of the organization is the work of shepherd management.

According to Robert C. Worley, the organizational world that includes the church and church-related organizations were once a gathering of family and friends, but has become a "gathering of strangers" in a complex and confusing relationship. (Worley, 1976) The gathering of strangers complicates the leadership role in organizations. It precipitates cultural conflict, misunderstandings, employee turnover, and loss of productive man-hours in the work of the organization. This creates a negative conditioning that affects leadership. (See Figure 8.1) Negative conditioning is a barrier to effective leadership.

This must be understood to accomplish or close the sale. History has recorded ample evidence that the medieval society which Western organizations so often pattern was created by monarchs, lords, barons and ruling clergy as they struggled with one another and the people for power and authority. Mankind is still victimized by old perspectives and patterns.

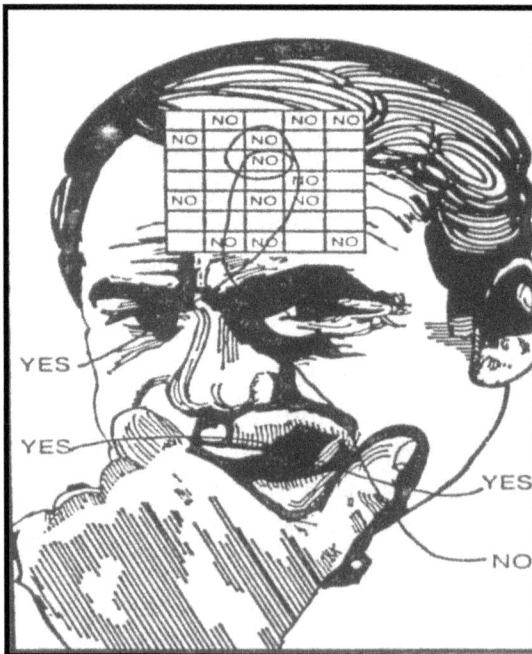

Figure 8.1-- *Negative Conditioning* is a formidable barrier to Direct Sales success. The problem is human engineering.

The power struggles of the past impact on the present

management and leadership difficulties. The struggle of ancient knights for a position of honor in the kingdom impacts on the battle for today's brass ring, blue ribbon or the hand of the boss' daughter. This striving for positional power and personal power in organizational life must be examined. The unexamined, hidden assumptions and the attitudes that accompany these struggles are extremely powerful in human life and in the organizational processes. (Figure 8.2)

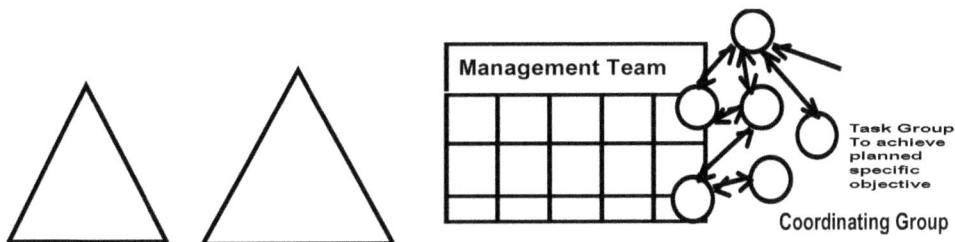

Sun-God Worship	19th-Century	ACCOUNTABILITY UNITS	
Feudal Lord Tribal Model	Industrial Religion & Military Systems	Twentieth Century Matrix Model	Twentieth-Century Industrial Network
Low discretion	←	→	High discretion
Low interdependence	←	→	High interdependence
One-way communication	←	→	Multiple direction
Private processes of decision making	←	→	Public processes of decision making
Evaluation lodged in one person, office or position	←	→	Review and evaluation mechanisms in a group
Coordination-integration in one person	←·······	·······>	Coordination-integration in a group, council, team
Coordination of organizational goals	← Standardization of each step	Planned sequence of steps →	Mutual adjustment-negotiation of planned
Nature of Environment	←	→	
	Static	Dynamic	

Different organizational structures are historically related to different leader and group behavior.

Figure 8.2

Many leaders still attempt to perform executive functions using patterns, style and tools of previous generations in a society that has long since developed other ways of seeing human organization and human behavior. Old world practices, European lifestyle, prevalent in society and adopted by Western organizations, are the crux of the problem today. There remains an "us and them" mentality that clouds the cultural perspective of persons, their interpersonal relationships, and their identity as individuals and as members of groups. Positional authority (power) cannot easily be translated into personal leadership (influence).

These perspectives are embedded in leadership styles and structures and processes of a bygone day. The old feudal system, for example, bespeaks a particular way of doing things established in a particular setting. Such impact has impressive power to persist long after the situation has changed. Individuals actually change more rapidly than do institutions. This is part of the problem.

The essence of an organization is in its people and their interrelationships; it is found in their relationships to leadership, to others, and to outsiders. Organizations must operate in the present, use contemporary tools as well as traditional language and inherent forms of thought to think creatively about the bottom line of profits and progress. The key to this is interpersonal relationships. Different organizational structures are historically related to different leader and group behavior.

Early in history the king or feudal lord wielded absolute power and control over the subjects in their domain. There was no exercise of discretionary authority from the top, the control over life and death was in the hands of one person. This gave way to a kind of top-down management with limited authority being given to various echelons of leaders. It was a ranked level of authority such as a military unit and was limited to one way communication. A private process of decision making existed and evaluation rested with one person or one office. One person controlled the coordination-integration of the people. Goals for the people were standardized for each step by a single person or entity. The people were not involved in even the private decisions that affected their personal and private lives.

This static period gave way to the dynamic development of accountability units that opened the way for a public process in decision making and review and evaluation mechanisms were placed in the hands of groups. A group, council, or team had input into the coordination and integration of the work and the people. This process led to coordinating groups and group tasking that precipitated mutual adjustment and negotiation of planed steps in an organization. Organizational goals became a planned and group process.

Persons actively construct their views of reality out of material available to them (what their perspective makes available). They create companies, groups, programs, coalitions of like-minded persons out of these perspectives. This is the group process which leaders must understand. It would be great if leadership had a "reveal code" key or button to push so all the hidden factors that impacts ones behavior would appear. Persons respond to what they see by using skills, tools and ideas which they think are appropriate to that view. Limited or inadequate perspectives may bring erroneous responses in the use of resources and in the choice of roles. Partial perspectives may bring erroneous responses in the use of resources and in the choice of roles. Partial perspectives do not allow persons to organize and mobilize personal resources or to alter ways of behavior to those that might be more effective or appropriate, thus the need for the free flow of information. (Figure 8.3 and 8.4.)

Leaders must see what actually exists. All leaders do not see with the same eyes. Each has a personal or professional point of view, often under-expressed and under-examined.

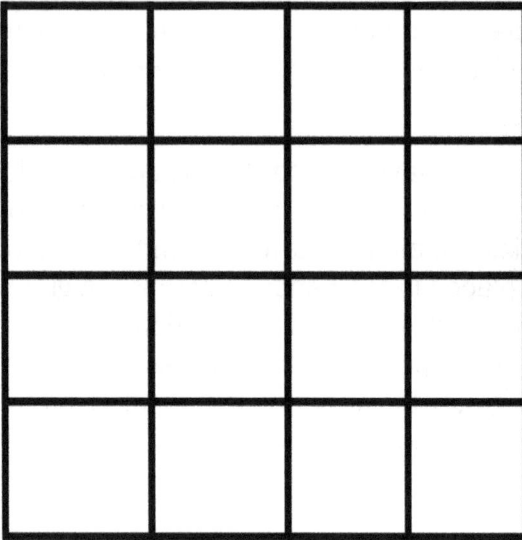

Figure 8.3–
How many squares do you see?

Figure 8.4– Whom do you see?

Leadership must see better what is going on in organizational life. What is happening to the people involved? What are the pressures on both leaders and followers? What is the quality and character of the work performed and how does this work fit into the scheme of things for the people and their goals?

Not only must leadership see, leaders must speak the truth about what they see. Leaders must talk about themselves and reflect together as people on the same team. Depth of perception comes when others help one to see himself and his relationship to others. Perspectives of persons are not consciously constructed; they are learned in families, churches and other community organizations. Perspectives are powerful because they determine how a person comes to see what is going on in his world...in his organization. Individuals are limited by their framework for seeing what is happening by their perspective. The managerial/technological society is marked by incorporated institutions and professional leadership. A brief outline of the sources of current organizational and managerial thinking would give perspective. (Figure 8.5)

Framework for viewing organizations

Organizational Theory comes from three major sources, all related, but traceable as separate strains of thought and processes. Each strain impacts on management and leadership. The first source is developed from viewing the structure. It is academic and theoretical—the formal discipline of organizational sociology.

Two names stand out in the development and elaboration of a conceptual framework for the study of organizations. Max Weber, early in this century listed the characteristics of classical organizational structure known as "bureaucracy."

SOURCE	VIEW	ACTION	RESULT
Organizational Sociology	Structure	Organized	Growth Development Change Division Decay Death
Human Relations Movement	Behavior	Human Behavior	Communicate Make Decisions
Business/ Industrial Management	Process	People doing some activity	Motivation Leadership Product Service Profits

Figure 8.5– Framework for viewing organizations

The four main characteristics of a classic bureaucracy or highly structured rational organization are:

1. Hierarchical authority structure
2. Clear division of labor
3. Functions abound by rules and precedents
4. Encumbering of officials based on technical qualifications and competence

Matrix is a non-bureaucratic model and groups together certain qualified persons for specific tasks and regroups to do other different tasks. Organizations doing relatively stable jobs in relatively stable ways tend to fall back on the classical ways of dealing with problems of accountability, competence, and order.

Systems Theory

Talcott Parsons, in his structural functional approach to the study of society, presented organizations in terms of "systems." An organization is a social grouping for a particular purpose. "System" is a broad word for "organization." Every social system is seen within its environment. It has boundaries of its own, which distinguish it from its environment, and mechanisms to maintain its boundaries and assure its continuity. Systems theory emphasizes relationships, and the effect of every part of a complex interrelated set of components and processes on every other part. It sees every system as a subsystem of a larger system. Each system, in turn, has internal subsystems of its own. Organizations and leaders must be concerned about a wider range of informal relationships and processes within its environment.

The second strain of organizational thinking views the people and behavior. It is the Human Relations Movement and deals with human potential. This movement has spawned or expressed itself in activities variously known as human relations training, sensitivity training, T-Groups, encounter groups, human potential development, change agency, applied behavioral science, and currently Organizational Development (O.D.). Most O.D. expresses itself through group dynamics known as Process Management. The human relations movement had its beginning in the early 1940's in the work of psychologist Kurt Lewin, whose interest in planned social change led to research in "group dynamics." Lewin developed a theory of "re-education," as an emotional as well as a cognitive process in which new values replace old ones.

Lewin's "force field theory" basically said if one could remove ten percent of the opposition to a cause it would be the same as putting ten times the force forward for the cause. In this regard, if ten percent of one's negative thoughts or feelings about a subject could be altered, it would be the same as empowering the person with ten times the energy to move forward using the present level of knowledge and strength.

The third strain views the processes. It comes from business and industrial management. It sees organizations in terms of the management of operations and achievement of goals. Guidance in dealing with concrete organizational problems (decision-making, personnel management, planning, budgeting-evaluation), comes from this area. Management by Objective (MBO) is a current contribution from this strain. Business and industrial organizations used "laboratory training" which became sensitivity training or T-Groups. As a method of bringing about organizational change through emphasis on the people in the organization, the reorientation of their values, and the facilitation of their self-fulfillment, the human relations movement continues to contribute to the business world. Abraham H. Maslow's "hierarchy of needs" with self-actualization at the top, is the heart of the movement's conception of human nature.

The main thrust is people and processes rather than structure. Enlightened management in business has shown great interest in the people who carry on its activity. Really, the interest is the outcome of this activity—products, sales, and profits. This is the primary focus.

A view of Formal and Informal Organization is seen in Figures 8.6, 8.7, and 8.8. Understanding the two types of organizations is essential to adequate leadership and corporate growth. In the formal, one develops the attitude of a Shepherd. Involvement with the informal aspect of an organization requires a Servant mindset. The Officer should be a Shepherd; the Leader must be a Servant. The function of a Shepherd is more related to management and the concept of Servant Leadership relates to influence in the administrative process.

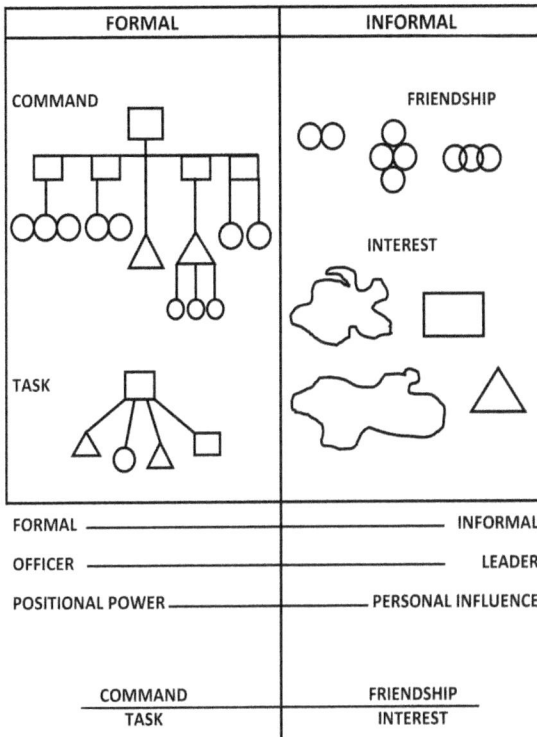

Figure 8.6--
Understanding the two types of organizations is essential to
adequate leadership and corporate growth.

It is a combination of both a shepherd mindset and a servant attitude that creates good management and leadership.

Figure 8.6 shows the dichotomy between formal and informal aspects of an organization. A dichotomy is a division into two contradictory parts, categories, or opinions. The word comes from the Greek, *dikhotomos*, meaning "to cut in two." It is this not so obvious division that leadership must understand. Since the formal is struggling to maintain the status quo and the informal striving to grow, leadership must deal simultaneously with both opinions.

Understanding this dichotomy is essential to the operation of an organization or institution. The severity of the division may be softened by a "shepherd's heart" in the formal side and a servants mindset on the informal side. However, the ability to lead (influence) is required to function adequately in either environment. Observe that the Task structure is made up of some of the same people in the Command structure and will have the same mind-set: to maintain the status quo. Notice should be taken that the Officer and Positional Authority is on the formal side and Leaders and Personal Influence on the informal side. The formal side lists both a Command and a Task structure while the informal side deals with friendship and interest.

Figure 8.6 clearly shows the formal and informal groups as they would appear if one had x-ray vision. Since no leader is equipped with such vision, there must be a clear understanding as to how this dichotomy functions in an organization. To ignore the functionality of the formal and the informal aspects of an organization would be to invite disaster. One should not see this structure as a threat, but view it as an opportunity to understand where people are and what they are doing.

Failure to have a functional awareness of the dichotomy can create real conflict between leadership and the people. Members of informal groups must find a place in the formal structure or they become discouraged and quietly absent themselves. This is called negative participation and is often ignored by leadership. Shepherds and servants must work together to find a comfortable place for all willing participants. This is mostly a factor with new or prospective members. Unless new people can clearly see how they fit into the overall organization, they will choose not to participate. Normally, an organization does not have sufficient data to understand the impact of negative participation on the comfort and health of the group or organization.

Each organization has to develop an absorbent pattern to retain people in a functional awareness. Otherwise a resistant pattern will develop that will result in negative participation in the life of the organization.

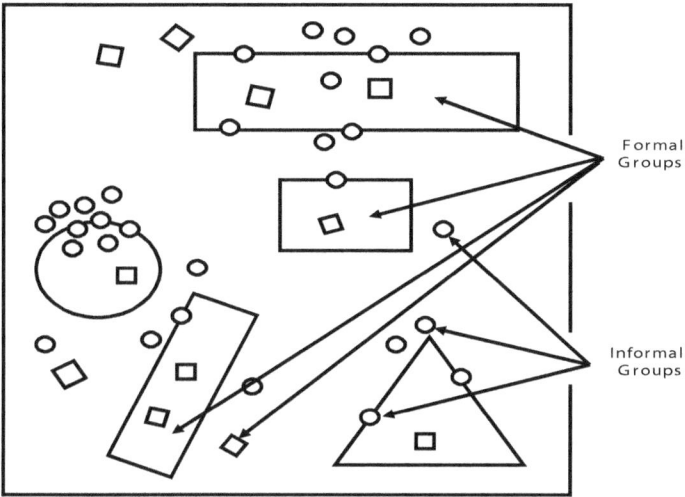

Figure 8.7– An x-ray of your organization

Figure 8.8–An absorbent pattern assures retention; a resistant pattern promotes turnover.

Study and Review Questions for Chapter Eight

1. Discuss structure, process and behavior.

2. What is meant by "a gathering of strangers?"

3. How are organizational structures historically related to different leader and group behavior?

4. Discuss the perspectives of persons.

5. Discuss the problem of negative conditioning with reference to management and leadership.

6. Enumerate the three ways of viewing organizations.

7. List the four main characteristics of a classic bureaucracy.

8. How does the "force field theory" relate to organizations?

CHAPTER NINE

Structuring Leadership Assumptions

Sometimes recognition of specific group behavior is difficult, especially when the leader becomes emotionally involved in the task. As previously stated, group maturity depends on individuals "giving up something" and for the leader this usually entails delegation of responsibility and authority along with some decision-making powers. This usually does not include giving up any accountability to higher authority.

Systematically Organized Knowledge

Based on assumption from the literature and decades of experience, custom, agreement, and/or formal and reasoned authority, a list of assumptions has been formulated for the study of management and leadership. A great deal of systematically organized knowledge exists in the field of management and leadership. Statements in the field differ based on basic assumptions or conjecture of the individual or discipline involved in the report. However, the assumptions are based on decades of experience together with agreed upon customs. Academics, managers, company officials, boards, directors, and many others have contributed to this experience base. Sadly, most of the literature neglects the early scriptural foundation that informs some of the key constructs that guide the behavior of leaders.

Some call this set of rules or principles, established by custom and agreement, "Laws." Others see the rules as a set of laws or statements devised to explain some phenomenon or class of phenomena and classify the list as "Theories." Still others see the rules as self-evident or universally recognized truth that is accepted without validation and identify the list as "Axioms." The following are simply worthy postulates or principles for the study or practice of the art or discipline of management and leadership.

Here is a list of assumptions that inform life-cycle management and leadership. Call them axioms, theories, assumptions or principles, they are all based on basics assumptions. A rose by any other name would smell the same. You be the judge!

There are seven assumptions governing leadership and understanding in group life and development. In contingency or situational theory, the following assumptions may be used as predictors for easing the difficulty of choosing the correct leadership behavior.

Assumption One
All groups begin at Stage 1.

Assumption Two
In order for a group to move from immaturity to maturity there must be a leader.

Assumption Three
There must be general agreement that the group has a meaningful reason for being in existence. Quite often committees and boards exist on paper only and have no clear-cut goals. The output of such groups is usually minimal and the group process immature.

Assumption Four

If the leader implies in even the slightest way that he does not support organizational goals then the group will not move toward maturity. The leader can force the issue through the task if the leader is task-oriented and can recognize where the group is on the maturity continuum and he can modify his own behavior accordingly.

Assumption Five

The group will reset towards immaturity whenever one of the following occurs:

New members are introduced to a mature (Stage 3 or 4) group. Group will probably reset to Stage 2 (STORM) until the role of the new individual is clearly defined and all conflicts are worked out. The mature group will be ready for this and have specific responsibilities and job descriptions ready for the newcomer. The leader must be prepared for the reset by expecting conflict. The leader must expect to move his behavior more to a task-oriented style initially. If enough new members are introduced then he must move all the way back to Quad I. The leader changes. A new leader virtually constitutes a new group and should begin in Quad I.

One of the worst mistakes for a leader is to take over a mature group and expect to start operating from Quad III or IV regardless of the degree of maturity observed under the old leader. The anxiety introduced to a group around peripheral things such as work hours, uniform standards, watch and job skill levels, "moonlighting," etc., is enough to drive the group to Stage 1 or 2.

The task changes. When a new task is introduced which re-quires a change of skills or behavior modification, reset is likely to occur. This is especially true when introducing con-cepts of equal opportunity that deal heavily in individual val-ues and personal emotions. This is where the true leader earns his pay. If the leader is unable to fully support the organizational goals and is unable to convey the spirit of unwavering personal commitment to the task, i.e., establishing a climate of equal opportunity, all that can be reasonably expected as output is a "paper drill" where the intent becomes to do the least amount possible in order to meet the minimum standards. Official (governmental) frustration at this passive-aggressive behavior results eventually in a quota system of equality, i.e., busing! Stage 2 (STORM) behavior by the group is manifested initially in a credibility check of the leader: "Is he for real?" This places the leader in a critical role if he has individual conflicts with the organizational goals. The leader who may have racist or sexist tendencies will probably find establishing a true climate of equal opportunity in his work group a difficult and unpleasant task.

The environment changes. A group will reset quite rapidly to an immature stage as a result of environmental change. (Example: a flight crew that is operating in Stage 3/4 suddenly encounters violent weather and crashes on a mountain top. Quad III leadership behavior must change to Quad I immediately in order to prevent panic and confusion. The leader (pilot in command) may even desire a change of leadership to someone more qualified in survival situations, possible even a passenger. However, the leader chooses to react, it is obvious that the "Coffee, tea or milk?" approach is inappropriate.)

In four reset examples described above, the degree of reset varies according to the original maturity of the group. (A more mature group will recognize the reset and compensate by coming to grips with the cause in order to return as quickly as possible to their advanced stage of maturity, i.e., the group will welcome a new member and immediately indoctrinate, educate, assess the experience and talents of and assign a role to a new member.)

Assumption Six

A sudden change in the behavior of the leader has the same effect as changing leaders. Therefore, a leader who realizes he/she is using Quad IV (low task – low relationship) behavior for a group obviously in Stage 2 development and switches suddenly to Quad II (high task – high relationship) should be prepared for an accelerated "STORM" period due to the anxiety caused by the new behavior. Things tend to get worse before they get better and the leader should seriously consider going all the way to Quad I in order to redefine the task and reset the operating perimeters and boundaries of the whole group.

Once Life-cycle Leadership is understood, the intuitive correctness of the assumptions is reinforced daily. For instance, with a quick diagnosis of an upset group it was painfully clear that the stage of maturity was Stage 2. "Frustrated, confused and upset" are words of "STORM." "No goals defined" was a strong indication that specific tasking was either not made very clear or not generally accepted. Who was the leader of this group? And what was that person doing? The group began moving towards maturity only after the group demanded clarification of the goals.

"Better guidance, direction and understanding by us of our tasks" suggests a critique by a good leader would have helped them through Stage 2. The lesson here is that if life-cycle leadership had been applied by a leader and had that leader demonstrated task-oriented Quad I behavior, like the GURU or the Drill Sergeant at boot camp, it is likely that the "wasteful day" could have been productive and the group led through Stage 1 and Stage 2 even with the emotional response to an undesirable task.

Assumption Seven

Common sense demands that leader behavior be governed by the needs and maturity of followers. Common sense demands that leaders use common sense. Yet, there is not enough common sense to go around. Take the simple thermostat on the wall. How does it work? What causes the heat or air conditioning to come on automatically? The next chapter provides data to assist with these questions.

Study and Review Questions for Chapter Nine

1. Discuss the first four assumptions of Contingency or Life-cycle Leadership.

2. How and why do groups reset toward immaturity?

3. What happens if a sudden change occurs in a leader's behavior?

4. How does common sense inform management and leadership?

5. Provide an example of leadership that distinguishes between form and function.

6. From your own knowledge and experience, discuss leadership in the light of both priorities and delegation.

7. Review the Jerusalem Council (Acts 15:1-35; 6:4-5). Describe the problem, the way it was solved and the significant results.

CHAPTER TEN

Social Change in Organizations

A Change Timetable

New leadership is normally in a hurry to make constructive changes, but reality must be faced squarely. Haste makes waste and premature change creates difficulties. It takes as long to change the culture of an organization as it took to create the present culture. Does this mean constructive change can never happen in an established organization? Of course, not! However, understanding the dynamics of cultural change does assist the appreciation for the small changes one sees and increases the tolerance for the gradual improvements that are taking place. Is the change moving fast enough? Of course, not! Again, the process can be nudged a little, but it cannot be pushed beyond the norms of a social change timetable without doing significant damage to the organization.

Constructive Change

Constructive change does not come easy. The organizational leadership team should make a contextual analysis of every aspect of the organization before initiating change. When the total constituency is viewed as a whole one sees a different picture than when an organization is broken down into parts: culture, traditions, groups, organizations, personnel, facilities, programs and services. Separating a whole into parts assists leaders in determining the nature, proportion, function, and relationship of various aspects of the organization in order to weave or knit together a new integrated entity that would demonstrate positive change without violating the basic institutional culture.

Affirmative Attitude Required

What is needed is not only affirmative attitude but also positive action. Everyone associated with the organization, past and present, must be seen as persons of worth with a potential productive contribution to the organization. Without this attitude positive change will become more difficult. Change is the natural process of organizational life and constructive change is built on the foundation of the labors of others. Those past labors must be respected and honored for the constructive part in the existing organization. Past leadership and the present constituency must understand that change is natural and usually necessary for an organization to progress toward the stated goals. Why must an organization change? An organization must change because times change, environments change, personnel changes, and the needs, desires, and wishes of future constituents change. Change must come, but it is best accepted in incremental elements rather than drastic changes that impact the culture of the organization.

All who live a normal lifespan see many changes, some positive and others negative, but change does come. Whether it is a change from quill to pen, parchment to paper, horse and buggy to the automobile, typewriter to computer, FAX and telephone to cell phones and the Internet, changes just keep coming and invade the comfort zone of many. However, discomfort can create movement and adjustment and seeing the value added aspect of change can cause acceptance.

For example, this author went kicking and screaming into the age of technology reluctant to leave my comfort zone. In the early days of the technology revolution my preference was the typewriter to the computer and the land line telephone to the wireless world. Finally embracing the value added aspects of the computer, cell phones and the wireless Internet as a way to increase productivity and stay in touch with global issues. Just as many "old timers" were reluctant to become trapped in the world-wide-web, a mechanism was developed to see the Internet as a positive value added to my work and worldview. To make the Internet work for me, new meaning was added to the (www); it became worship–wellness–wealth. Why? How? Worship reminded me of the vertical response to the "worth and value" of God in my life and work; wellness suggested a healthy lifestyle, and wealth pointed to adequate resources for family and kingdom work. This provided affirmation that constructive change could work and produce small changes in the cultural fabric of both individuals and organizations.

Change Has a Life of Its Own

Changes in an organization is at first a natural occurrence, but change seems to multiply and as changes increase more disapproving feelings are expressed by constituents. Change then begins to take on a life of its own and grows exponentially until the whole culture or the organization is significantly changed. This may cause a clear break with past constituency and cause negative participation by previous customers or supporters.

Redirection of Attitudes

It would be good if everyone could accept constructive change as a normal part of organizational life. Communicating changes as a value added process to the organization is the best way to assure support. This level of communication will not happen until there is a redirection of attitudes at the leadership level of an organization. Top level decisions are not made in a vacuum. Transparency is required and constituents need to clearly see the antecedent case that produced the need for change in existing projects, programs, or services. Arbitrary changes will be resisted, but transparency can transcend most opposition to positive change.

Patience is a Virtue

The more the leadership team behavior becomes responsible and accountable to the constituency the more effective proposed changes will be accepted. Leaders must never feel they are the lords over God's heritage, but must think of themselves as servants of the constituency. Patience is the ability to remain under pressure with a positive attitude until certain things are accomplished. This is why the Ancient Greeks called the sick folk who came to see a physician "patients," because they had to remain under the pressure of an illness until the medical practitioner was able to treat the infirmity. Patience means a calm endurance of difficulties, inconvenience or delay until better conditions arrive. Patience is identified by tolerance of a situation that is unacceptable; it is developed by misfortune and suffering, strengthened by enduring the present, magnified by uncomplaining hope, and characterized by a patience extended toward those who resist change.

Freeze-Frame Thinking

Since positive change takes place at the level of ideas and values, ideology is the common ground of constructing positive change in an organization. Ideology is composed of philosophy and theology and it is where ideas and values come together. Often the constituency and the leadership team of an organization are stuck in a prison of previous patterns a kind of freeze-frame thinking constructed by snap shots of the past. It is precisely this that requires the transparency and openness when communicating the elements of change and the rational for the change. Most individuals are comfortable when the present overlaps the past and contains some of the basic elements from a familiar comfort zone. This is why leadership must be relational to all the constituency and publics of the organization.

The Change Agent process

A leader must decide whether to behave as a catalyst or become an agent for change in the organization. A catalyst may speed up the change process, but will not be changed personally. This can be a serious drawback to full cooperation in any organized group. The members of an organization expect the leadership to grow, develop, and change over time. They also expect this change to be positive. To remain the same and not change with the times to mature with the group creates the "left behind syndrome" and creates an urgency to act by leadership. This rush to action usually creates more difficulty that it solves. All action should be planned and understood behavior. There must be clearly expressed goals or reasons for all acts by leadership. Otherwise the people will question the legitimacy of the leader's behavior.

On the other hand, when a leader behaves as change agent, there is change on the part of the leader. As the situation changes and the people grow, the leader develops along with them. The concept of "team" is realized and things get done in an efficient and effective manner. Consider Force Field Analysis using Lewin's Force Field Theory. The leader must do a situation audit before acting. What are the difficulties that must be overcome? How can the opposition be lessened? The force field construct reminds the leader that if only ten percent of the opposition can be removed it is the same as putting ten times the force forward for an issue, cause, program, or project. With this in mind, all individuals in leadership should understand how to do a situation audit.

It requires less effort, time, and funds to remove ten percent of the opposition than to increase ten times the force forward. To move equal and opposing forces, a leader can take one of two approaches: (1) Increase the pressure ten times or, (2) concentrate on removing ten percent of the opposing forces. This is where the situation audit assists the leader in determining the way forward.

There are seven steps in the situation audit. One may better understand the concept and construct of the Situation Audit by completing steps 1 – 7 in a practice session. It is better to learn the procedure dealing with a hypothetical problem than to attempt a situation audit the first time under "combat conditions."

Do a Situation Audit by completing 1 – 7

1. State where you are and where you want to be:

2. State all the forces that will assist you in making the desired change:

3. State all the forces that will <u>hinder</u> you from making the desired change:

4. Now analyze, prioritize and plot these forces on a grid:

5. Now brainstorm for possible "action strategy" options:

6. Now select and further plan the best of these options:

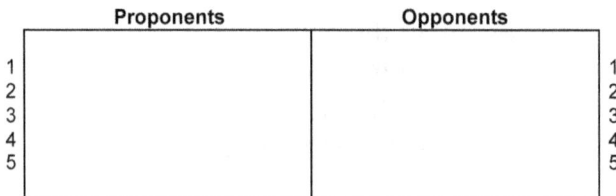

	Proponents	Opponents	
1			1
2			2
3			3
4			4
5			5

Figure 10.1–

Place the plan into the calendar. Give yourself plenty of lead-time for major change. Watch out for excessive change in too short of a period.

Change Respondent Analysis

Following a situational analysis where the proponents and opponents have been identified, there must be a process to change the attitude, or predisposition to act, of the respondents. To do this each individual must be classified as a radical, progressive, conservative or traditionalist in relationship to their attitude about change. Use the diagram below to assist your thinking about this issue. Remember, individuals change more rapidly than groups, and groups change faster than organizations. Concentrate on changing individuals. These changed individuals can slowly change the groups of which they are a part. As the groups change, the organization can move toward the cultural or social change that is required for the organization or institution to move forward.

A Change Respondent Analysis can assist in planning a way forward. This way may be "over the hill and around the bend" but it is the only way to move an organization or institution in a new direction or speed up the process of change that is required to meet the present needs of the people and the organization.

CHANGE PROGRAM RESPONDENTS

Proponents		Opponents	
+ +	+	−	− −
Radicals	Progressives	Conservatives	Traditionalists
I	II	III	IV
Proponents of extreme change	Proponents of moderate change	Disposed to maintaining existing conditions	Opponents of any change

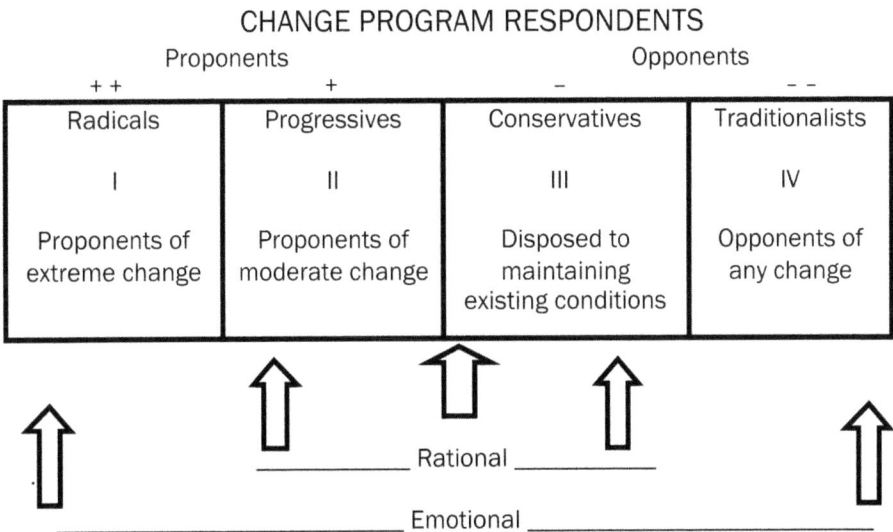

Rational

Emotional

Figure 10.2–

- Identify the Radicals
- Identify the Progressives
- Identify the Conservatives
- Identify the Traditionalists

CLASSIFICATION OF CHANGE ATTITUDES

RADICALS	PROGRESSIVES	CONSERVATIVES	TRADITIONALISTS
Proponents of extreme change	Proponents of moderate change	Disposed to maintaining existing conditions	Opponents of any change
RADICALS	PROGRESSIVES	CONSERVATIVES	TRADITIONALISTS
Proponents of extreme change	Proponents of moderate change	Disposed to maintaining existing conditions	Opponents of any change

Figure 10.3–

- Who are they?
- How will you deal with each group?

Study and Review Questions for Chapter Ten

1. Compare a catalyst and a change agent in management and leadership.

2. Discuss a force field analysis.

3. What is a change respondent analysis?

4. Discuss the attitude of radicals, progressives, conservatives, and traditionalists in relation to change.

5. How would you deal with each group?

6. Read the Book of Nehemiah. Identify the nature of the problem and the way the problem was solved. Nehemiah used both organizational and administrative skills that included both the human element and divine dimensions. They are blended carefully in the narrative and are difficult to separate, but they are both there. Discuss Nehemiah's problem, the solution and the results together with the skills used. Include the human element and the divine dimension.

CHAPTER ELEVEN

Subject Syllabus for Study

MANAGEMENT AND LEADERSHIP

Professor: Hollis L. Green, ThD, PhD

Subject Description

This subject considers the formal and informal aspects of administration and organization with emphasis on the life-cycle leadership and application to the structure, processes, and behavior of organized groups.

Subject Syllabus for Study
Subject Objectives

Developmental readings should be guided by these objectives.

A.	To discover the formal and informal aspects of organizations.

B.	To focus on useful assumptions concerning structure, process and behavior in organizational life.

C.	To obtain a perspective on organizations and identity.

D.	To grasp a perspective of personal and organizational goals as they relate to forms of power and involvement of persons.

E.   To enable leaders to use contemporary tools as well as traditional structure and language to think about tasks and relationships.

F.   To increase leader effectiveness and understanding of task and relationship problems.

G.   To see environment as a source of anxiety and promise.

Subject Outline

I   Sympathetic Leadership Cybernetics
A.   A Sympathetic System
B.   Synergy
C.   Ability to Influence People
D.   Essential Leadership Traits
    1. How Organizations Develop and Grow
    2. Vision
    3. Courage
    4. Integrity
    5. Perseverance
    6. Collegial Model of Leadership

II.   S-Curve of Organizational Growth
A.   S-Curve of Growth
B.   Stages of Organizational Development
C.   A Cybernetic Process – the Thermostat
D.   The Small Ball Theory
E.   Leadership and Patience
F.   Information Sharing Patterns

III. Situational Dynamic Relationships
A.   Functional leadership is understood in terms of dynamic relationships.
B.   The "Time" factor in leadership
C.   McGregor's "Theory X and Theory Y" introduced leadership attitudes

D.   Theory Z represents an overall positive
       attitude of the leader
E.   Attitudinal leadership requires a consideration
       of both task and relationship.
F.   Berne's Transactional Analysis

IV.   Stages of Maturity and Behavior
A.   Life-cycle offers a choice of styles of
       leadership
B.   Life-cycle Theory suggests that group
       development towards maturity has four
       stages:

       1. Dependent - FORM STAGE
       2. Counter Dependent – STORM STAGE
       3. Independent – NORM STAGE
       4. Interdependent – PERFORM STAGE

C.   Leaders must make behavior modifications as
           the group matures:
       1.   FORM – High Task/Low Relationship
            (Telling)
       2.   STORM – High Task/High Relationship-
            (Selling)
       3.   NORM – High Task/Low Task-
            (Participating)
       4.   PERFORM – Low Relationship/Low Task-
            (Delegating)

D.   The key to adequate leadership is the
       determination of group maturity
E.   The most universal application of Life-cycle
       Theory occurs in the parent-child relationship
F.   The educational system is based on a
       development from high structure or no
       structure
G.   A group moves from immaturity to maturity
       through four stages:

    1. Mutual Acceptance – Dependent
    2. Decision Making – Counter Dependent
    3. Constructive – Independent
    4. Cohesiveness/Content – Interdependent

H.   Life-cycle Theory proposes that the leader's behavior should move systematically through four stages:

    1. High Task – Low Relationship
    2. High Task – High Relationship
    3. Low Task – High Relationship
    4. Low Task – Low Relationship

I.   Life-cycle leadership hinges on the interaction of task and relationship.

    1. Task Behavior
    2. Relationship Behavior

J.   A leader's influence is determined by both qualities and perception.

V.   Shepherd Management
A.   Nature of sheep and shepherding
B.   Shepherd and the Sheepfold
C.   Shepherd and the Bell Sheep
D.   Shepherd Management

VI.   Servant Leadership
A   The Essence of Leadership
B   Management of a Household
C.   Human Aspiration for Authority
D.   A Creation of Human Culture
E.   Funds Available Budget
F.   Volunteers vs. Hirelings
G.   Judgment Based on false Assumptions
H.   Educating Future Leaders
I.   Positional Authority vs. Personal Influence

J.   Servant Leadership

VII.   Source of Divine Viewpoint
A.   Three Basic Institutions
B.   The family produces individuals
C.   The Community protects individuals
D.   The organized church preserves individuals
E.   Organisms, Groups, and Organizations
F.   Organizational Socialization
G.   Individual Empathy
H.   Management and leadership Autonomy
I.   Confidence is a Factor
J.   Purpose, Objectives, Goals, and Standards
K.   Planning Process determines Action
L   Three Reasons for Planning
M.   The Planning Cycle

VIII.   Separate Strains of Thought and Process_
A.   Negative conditioning is a barrier to leadership
B.   Words of the past do not inform the present
C.   An "us and them" mentality clouds the cultural
        perspective of persons
D.   Power cannot be easily translated into influence
E.   Organizational structures are historically related to
        different leader and
F.   group behavior
G.   Leaders must see what actually exists
H.   Leaders must speak the truth about what they see
I.   Perspectives of persons are not consciously
        constructed
J.   Organizational theory comes from three major
        sources:

        1. Organizational Sociology
        2. Human Relations Movement
        3. Business/Industrial Management

K.   Formal and informal aspects of organization

IX.   Structuring Leadership Assumptions
A.   Assumption One – all groups begin at Stage I
B.   Assumption Two – there must be a leader for a group
      to move toward maturity
C.   Assumption Three – there must be general
      agreement that the group has a meaningful reason
      for being in existence
D.   Assumption Four – if the leader implies in even the
      slightest way a lack of support for organizational
      goals, the group will not move toward maturity
E.   Assumption Five – the group will reset towards
      immaturity whenever one of the following occurs:

      1. New members are introduced to a mature group
      2. The leader changes
      3. The task changes
      4. The environment changes
      5. The task changes
      6. The environment changes

F.   Assumption Six – a sudden change in the behavior of
      the leader has the same effect as changing leaders
G.   Assumption Seven – common sense demands that
      leader behavior be governed by the needs and
      maturity of the follower

X.   Social Change in Organizations
A.   The Change Agent process
B.   Change Respondent Analysis
C.   Change Program Respondents
D.   Leadership cybernetics
E.   Classification of Change Attitudes
F.   Leadership – a cybernetic approach

CHAPTER TWELVE

Subject Resources and Bibliography

Suggested Reading

Marable, M. (1998). *Black Leadership*. New York: Columbia University Press.

Dubois, S. C. (2000). *Black Social Change.* Westport, CT: Greenwood Publishing Group, Inc.

Rost, J. C. (1993). *Leadership for the Twenty-first Century.* NY: Praeger.

Gardner, H. & Larkin, E. *Leading Minds: An Anatomy of Leadership. NY:* Basic Books.

Peterson, Marvin W. Chaffee, Ellein E., White, Theodore H. (Eds.), Organization and Governance in Higher Education. Fourth Edition. Simon & Schuster. (1991). (See Chapter: "Alternative Models of Governance in Higher Education."

Electronic Bibliography on Administration and Leadership (Questia)

Books can be found by going into a library web site and clicking "Online Libraries." Then click "Libraries" and scroll to the "Electronic Resources" section. Click on "Questia" and follow directions given to you from the Library Orientation regarding accessing that electronic database.

Leadership and Organization: A Behavioral Science Approach.
   Contributors: Robert Tannenbaum - author, Irving R.
   Weschler - author, Fred Massarik - author. Publisher:
   McGraw-Hill. Place of Publication: New York. Page
   Number: v. Publication Year: 1961.

Publication Title: Transformational Leadership: Industrial,
   Military, and Educational Impact. Contributors: Bernard
   M. Bass - author. Publisher: Lawrence Erlbaum
   Associates. Place of Publication: Mahwah, NJ. Page
   Number: iii. Publication Year: 1998.

Publication Title: The Study of Leadership. Contributors: C.
   G. Browne - editor, Thomas S. Cohn - editor. Publisher:
   Interstate Printers and Publishers. Place of Publication:
   Danville, IL. Page Number: iii. Publication Year: 1958.

Publication Title: Leading Minds: An Anatomy of Leadership.
   Contributors: Howard Gardner - author, Emma Laskin -
   author. Publisher: Basic Books. Place of Publication: New
   York. Page Number: iii. Publication Year: 1996.

Publication Title: When Women Lead: Integrative Leadership
   in State Legislatures. Contributors: Cindy Simon
   Rosenthal - author. Publisher: Oxford University Press.
   Place of Publication: New York. Page Number: iii.
   Publication Year: 1998.

Publication Title: Capturing the Heart of Leadership:
   Spirituality and Community in the New American
   Workplace. Contributors: Gilbert W. Fairholm - author.
   Publisher: Praeger Publishers. Place of Publication:
   Westport, CT. Page Number: iii. Publication Year: 1997.

Publication Title: Leadership in Higher Education: A Handbook
   for Practicing Administrators. Contributors: Bob W.
   Miller - editor, Robert W. Hotes - editor, Jack D. Terry -
   editor. Publisher: Greenwood Press. Place of Publication:
   Westport, CT. Page Number: iii. Publication Year: 1983.

Publication Title: Facilitating Training Groups: A Guide to
Leadership and Verbal Intervention Skills. Contributors:
Susan A. Wheelan - author. Publisher: Praeger Publishers.
Place of Publication: New York. Page Number: iii.
Publication Year: 1990.

Publication Title: Leadership for the Twenty-First Century .
Contributors: Joseph C. Rost - author. Publisher: Praeger
Publishers. Place of Publication: New York. Page Number:
iii. Publication Year: 1993.

Publication Title: Motivation, Emotions, and Leadership: The
Silent Side of Management. Contributors: Richard C.
Maddock - author, Richard L. Fulton - author. Publisher:
Quorum Books. Place of Publication: Westport, CT. Page
Number: iii. Publication Year: 1998.

Publication Title: Organizational Behavior: The State of
the Science. Contributors: Jerald Greenberg - editor.
Publisher: Lawrence Erlbaum Associates. Place of
Publication: Hillsdale, NJ. Page Number: iii. Publication
Year: 1994.

Publication Title: Organizational Participation: Myth and
Reality. Contributors: Frank Heller - author. Publisher:
Oxford University. Place of Publication: Oxford. Page
Number: iii. Publication Year: 1998.

Publication Title: Organizational Transformation: Approaches,
Strategies, Theories. Contributors: Amir Levy - author, Uri
Merry - author. Publisher: Praeger Publishers. Place of
Publication: New York. Page Number: iii. Publication Year:
1986.

Publication Title: Applied Organizational Communication:
Perspectives, Principles, and Pragmatics. Contributors:
Thomas E. Harris - author. Publisher: Lawrence Erlbaum
Associates. Place of Publication: Hillsdale, NJ. Page
Number: iii. Publication Year: 1993.

Publication Title: Personnel Selection and Assessment:
Individual and Organizational Perspectives. Contributors:
Heinz Schuler - editor, James L. Farr - editor, Mike
Smith - editor. Publisher: Lawrence Erlbaum Associates,
Publishers. Place of Publication: Hillsdale, NJ. Page
Number: iii. Publication Year: 1993.

Publication Title: Information Seeking: An Organizational
Dilemma. Contributors: J. David Johnson - author.
Publisher: Quorum Books. Place of Publication: Westport,
CT. Page Number: iii. Publication Year: 1996.

Publication Title: Productivity Measurement and
Improvement: Organizational Case Studies. Contributors:
Robert D. Pritchard - editor. Publisher: Praeger Publishers.
Place of Publication: Westport, CT. Page Number: iii.
Publication Year: 1995.

Publication Title: Sacred Companies: Organizational Aspects
of Religion and Religious Aspects of Organizations.
Contributors: N. J. Demerath III - editor, Peter Dobkin Hall
- editor, Terry Schmitt - editor, Rhys H. Williams - editor.
Publisher: Oxford University Press. Place of Publication:
New York. Page Number: iii. Publication Year: 1998.

Journal Articles (ProQuest)

These articles can be found by going into an online Library."
Then click "Libraries" and scroll up until you find "Proquest."
Double-click on "Proquest."

Women managers and gendered values. *Women's Studies
in Communication*; Los Angeles; Winter 2000; Diane Kay
Sloan; Kathleen J Krone.

Leadership and business ethics: Does it matter? Implications
for management. *Journal of Business Ethics*; Dordrecht;
Jul 1999; A L Minkes; M W Small; S R Chatterjee.

Maintain excellence, cut risk. *Journal of Accountancy*; New York; Jan 2003; Patrick J McDonnell.

Improving organizational communication and cohesion in a health care setting through employee-leadership exchange. *Human Organization*; Washington; Fall 2002; Elisa J Sobo; Blair L Sadler.

The teaching of leadership, cooperation, and communication in a class entitled: Management of counseling programs. *TCA Journal*; Austin; Spring 2002; Dennis M Pelsma; Patrica J Neufeld.

Participative management and job satisfaction: Lessons for management leadership. *Public Administration Review*; Washington; Mar/Apr 2002; Soonhee Kim.

A team building intervention program: Application and evaluation with two university soccer teams. *Journal of Sport Behavior*; Mobile; Dec 2001; Mike Voight; John Callaghan.

The Aldo Leopold leadership program: Training environmental scientists to be civic scientists. *Science Communication*; Thousand Oaks; Sep 2001; Barry D Gold.

Knowledge management and leadership opportunities for technical communicators. *Technical Communication*; Washington; Nov 2000; Corey Wick.

Empowering our own: Peer leadership training for a drop-in center. *Psychiatric Rehabilitation Journal*; Boston; Fall 2000; Kia J Bentley.

Values in decision-making processes: Systematic structures of J. Habermas and N. Luhmann for the appreciation of responsibility in leadership. *Journal of Business Ethics*; Dordrecht; Sep 2000; Eberhard Schnebel.

Management communication for the new millennium. *Management Communication Quarterly : McQ*; Thousand Oaks; Aug 2000; Elizabeth A More; Harry T Irwin.

Four additional books may assist those teaching or taking this course. The following four books, and others published by The Press, may be ordered with free shipping within the USA from www.globaledadvance.org/bookstore.

Transformational Leadership in Education

ISBN 978-0-9801674-6-7 $19.95

AUTHOR: Hollis L. Green, ThD, PhD

The transformational aspect of education is a strengths-based approach that acknowledges the background and capacity of the staff, the teacher, and the learner. The curriculum becomes a vehicle to move the learner in a positive direction based on prior knowledge and maturity. This book provides a structure to nurture relationships between the system oversight, the principal, the teachers, the students, and the parents in a four-step model known as form/storm/norm/perform. This path to positive change is needed to adopt, deploy and ultimately bring about constructive change in the teaching/learning process. All involved in the educational arena must feel comfortable with the process and be open to new thinking and learning patterns for beneficial change to become a reality. In this age of technology and 24/7/365 exposure to global issues, to accomplish the transformational changes required to advance the teaching/learning process, the educational system must move beyond pedagogic methods to more advanced interactive learning designs based on the maturity of the learner.

Interpreting an Author's Words

ISBN 978-0-9801674-8-1 $19.95

AUTHOR: Hollis L. Green, ThD, PhD

Refine study and writing skills by understanding the written word. The difficulty in understanding the written word is not the vagueness of the composition, but the elusiveness of the author. A basic problem in understanding an author's words relates to the language and culture. When words or thoughts are translated from one language and a particular culture to another the meaning changes. These changes often go unnoticed and individuals apply a current definition to the words. In fact the meaning of words is in people. This could be the reason English/European students read authors rather than subjects. Knowing the orientation of the author and the background, philosophy, and purpose of the composition increases the understanding of the written document. So rooted in the earliest awareness of a need for knowledge and the continuing search by generations of thinkers, the systematic process of investigation emerge, in spite of the hurdles of vested interests and lack of support from the general populous. The present concept of scientific methodology began to form during medieval times and developed into a full body of concepts and constructs in the modern age. As humans wrote down their observations, the effort to understand what was written began. To understand and interpret different aspects of human existence, various groups of scholars began to devise different schemes, but all used the basic method of inquiry.

Remedial and Surrogate Parenting

ISBN 978-1-935434-41-2 $19.95

AUTHOR: Hollis L. Green, ThD, PhD

Just like footprints, each child is different and age-specific care is required to guide their footsteps. This book provides information for all who provide care for children and supplies basic guidance to make surrogate parenting work. The text is a study and reference guide for foster parents, caregivers in children's homes, as well as a basic guide for parents. There is a relationship between the attitude, knowledge, and behavior of caregivers and the quality of care for growing children. Custodial childcare is not a basket of bad apples that need to be culled from society. Rather it is a cradle of socialization filled with precious fruit of the womb picked from the tree of life to be preserved for society.

How to Build a Better Spouse Trap

ISBN 978-1-935434-45-0 $19.95

AUTHOR: Hollis L. Green, ThD, PhD

How to choose a mate, learn from your mistakes, stay married, and teach others to break the cycle of dysfunctional relationships The present system is designed to catch and ensnare a mate whether that mate ever becomes a spouse is doubtful. Part of the difficulty with failed marriages is that the participants soon feel trapped in a bad relationship. Why do they feel trapped? When the dating game is over and the spouse that set the trap is tired of the old party time, they want out. They start looking elsewhere for sensual excitement, but there are children and financial obligations that are not easy to evade. The more trapped the individual feels the more their behavior becomes animalistic and violent. The relationship becomes sadistic and abusive and the spouse and children suffer. One more marriage relationship is headed for the dung heap. Another marriage has been sundered. There must be a better way! Why can't we be more objective in mate selection?

About the Author

A Distinguished Professor of Education and Social Change, Hollis Lynn Green has taught at graduate level for more than three decades. A Diplomate in the Oxford Society of Scholars, he has authored 40 plus books and numerous articles, served pastorates in five states, and lectured in over 100 countries. Dr. Green was the founding President (1981) and Chancellor (1991) of Oxford Graduate School (www.ogs.edu), and founded OASIS University (2002) in Trinidad, W.I. (www.osasisedu.org). In 2007, he launched Global Educational Advance, Inc. as a logical outgrowth of his ministry through education. His books can be purchased through www.GlobalEdAdvance.org/bookstore) as well as other book distribution sources such as Amazon, etc. Bookstores and suppliers order through Ingram.

SYMPAHETIC LEADERSHIP CYBERNETICS
Serving Organizations Through
Shepherd Management and Servant Leadership

ISBN 978-1-935434-52-8

Hollis L. Green, ThD, PhD

GlobalEdAdvancePress™
www.globaledadvance.org

www.ingramcontent.com/pod-product-compliance
Lightning Source LLC
Chambersburg PA
CBHW051722090426
42738CB00010B/2045